OUR
VOTES
MATTER

By Eric Scott

CONTENTS

****

INTRODUCTION

VOTE

verb

1: to express one's views in response to a poll; especially :
to exercise a political franchise

2 : to express an **opinion**...
~Merriam-Webster Dictionary

Are you ready to express your opinion in a way that truly matters? Are you ready take the sort of action that really makes an impact? Stay with me as I candidly share why your vote can bring about change for your home, your family, your community, your state, and your nation.

There has been much talk from politicians, and so-called community leaders about why it is important to get out and vote. While it is commendable, there still has not been any significant action at the polls that manifest the sort of change to particular issues that matter to us. In this book, Our Vote Matters, I will like to talk with you about why each vote in the African American community is vital if we really want to see change from the White House to our door step.

****

Our Votes Matters *by Eric Scott is a timely, and relevant text which serves to effectively reach into the African American community to disclose the power each voter possesses, and encourage them to harness that power to secure eventual change in the nation, particularly in areas which affect us directly.*

Various voting campaigns, and legal initiatives have fallen short of securing the return on voter activity that represents Black minorities.

Why is this? One may ask.

In this book Eric Scott speaks frankly with his community, in a relatable voice, to expose how a lack of voting contributes to continued oppression from the "powers that be".

He reveals strategies used by politicians, including the "Bait and Switch", to blind African Americans from the bigger picture, of a better quality of life. **Our Vote Matters** *also informs on how choosing to not participate with voting correlates to the breakdown of the family structure, one's neighborhood, jobs, health care, investment and more.*

Eric surveys the traditional African American leadership, and minority organizations whose voices have softened, and whom have strayed from bringing about change where it is truly needed. He questions their effectiveness, and their agenda, as well as educates on where true effective community leadership should emerge from. Eric's philosophy is fresh and "outside the box".

This is not your usual literature about voting, or politics either. Eric has initiated a down-to-earth conversation to stir his friends, and neighbors nationwide to bring about change where it truly matters.

Amidst all the unfortunate, and critical events occurring in the news around the country; beyond protests, boycotts, and marches, if the laws do not change, then it is all for nought.

So from a fellow community member, and Administration of Justice expert, with an insider vantage point, Eric Scott has penned this conversation to reassure Black America that together, One vote...Our BLACK Vote equals real Permanent, and Legal CHANGE!

****

CHAPTER 1

VOTING - It's *Your Right*

Yes! It IS your right to vote.

You have probably heard it said before - time and time again - and have may have let it glide over your consciousness without careful consideration. However, take some time to imagine---imagine the selfless sacrifice--- imagine the physical pain as a result of brutal violence--- imagine the fight in their spirits as they thought about you. Yes, I am talking about your forefathers. The people who looked just like you, and carried your name, and had the same blood running through their veins. They dove in, and endured discomfort, and even injury to their bodies, so that you and I can freely cast our vote in order to *participate* in the decisions made in national, and local government.

Do you really think that your grandparents, great grandparents, and other ancestors willing tolerated bodily harm fighting for the right to vote, if they believed that it did not make a difference to their quality of life?...No! They knew that they would have a say. They knew that they would actively be shaping their family's future when they gained the chance to make their vote COUNT.

VOTING - It's *Your Privilege*

Check this out. The United States is the only country where we vote for City Council members, Mayors, School Board officials, State Commissioners, Judges, Lieutenant Governor, Governor, Senators, and Representatives, on the state level. Then, we also elect the Vice-President, and President on the national level.

That is correct! We have this privilege built into our democracy, yet we do not use it to our full advantage. For *every* issue that impacts your neighborhood. For *every* issue that impacts your state. For *every* issue that impacts your country, you have the ability, within your hands, to influence the outcome of the decisions made regarding it.

Let's take Britain for example. The citizens of the United Kingdom only vote nationally for their representatives to Parliament. Can you picture a United States of America where your privilege to vote is reduced to **only** selecting your representatives to Congress? Can you imagine a way of life where you are only allowed to elect just one single official, whether local or national, and all the other options were taken away? You have the opportunity to elect individuals to a variety of offices, at various levels, while million others who are citizens of other countries don't have anywhere near the same privilege.

So let's pause for a minute. Think---Ponder---Contemplate about the various areas within your own community, state, and nation where you can shake things up with your vote.

Whatever issues are on the table at your children's school-You can, shake it up!

Whatever issues are on the table within your community-You can, shake it up!

Whatever issues are on the table within your city-You can, shake it up!

Whatever issues are on the table within your state-You can, shake it up!

Whatever issues are on the table within your nation-You can, shake it up!

It is important to be ProActive instead of reactive - Shake It Up!

****

CHAPTER 2

Sleight of Hand

As a child, do you remember any magic tricks that you saw performed? What about more recently? Do you re-call observing his (or her) wizardry, and craftiness as one hand is used to distract the audience, while the other hand does the so-called "magic"? This approach is commonly described as the *Sleight-of-Hand* application. There really isn't any "magic" involved, except the illusionist intelligently making the best use of the natural tendency for the eye to be directed towards the obvious, and miss the important details also cryptically taking place.

Politicians also subscribe to this method in order to distract society with made-up issues while the real issues are masked. Colin Harris, Professor Emeritus, at Mercer University provides an example in his 2013, EthicsDaily.com article:

"While leaders raise the specter of "Big Government" coming to take away our freedom, we are effectively distracted from the realization that "Big Money" already has."

I would also like to draw your attention to another recent political *Sleight-of-Hand*. I'm sure that you've heard about the widely shared Student Forgiveness Plan announced by the Obama administration. While an honorable concept, this plan largely benefits those who've acquired loans from private institutions? Why does that matter? Well consider this: The majority of individuals in the African-American community who acquire loans to provide their children...our children...with a higher education are generally reliant on state, and or, federal loans. Statistically private loans often tend to escape us. Therefore, there is no real or tangible, even significant deal here for us. Where is the sort of forgiveness that will truly make a difference to our pockets, and credit score, for that matter? Student loans drives down our scores which causes a domino effect in all other areas of our lives as a community.

Just how many other issues have politicians, and other leaders used to distract us - the voting population. You may be surprised to learn, that it is a hefty amount. It is a common place political strategy. However, who does it benefit? - If you have answered, *the politicians* you are most certainly correct! It is a tactic used to pull the wool over our eyes, in order to further their own agenda.

Now it is critical that we not only become aware of this, but also educate ourselves, and insist upon, and push an agenda that benefits *us*-our community. We can't afford to continue to believe that the political leaders hold all the cards, or even have our best interest at the forefront of their minds. Look a little closer. You have a decent deck of cards in your hand. *Now, together, let's learn how to play them strategically.*

I would like to further identify, and break down, three specific methods politicians use to execute their *Sleight of Hand* device. They are, Bait and Switch, Placate and the colloquial term; Trickology.

Bait and Switch

Let's dive straight into breaking down the first strategy used by politicians to reel us in-pun intended. The *Bait and Switch* method is pretty simple, yet executed in such a manner that the majority of us get hooked-pun intended-easily.

The Merriam-Webster dictionary defines *Bait* as the following;
To put a piece of food on (a hook) or in (a trap) in order to attract and catch fish or animals.

We all get that. Some of us have gone fishing, for actual fish. Others have devised our own type of bait to impress someone, and attract a romantic partner, or even used *Bait* to secure the job of your dreams. What plan have you devised in the last few years, or even just yesterday, to reel someone in? To trap someone for your own benefit. You know you've done it. Heck! I know I did as a youngster. Whatever your plan, devise, whether innocent or a little more tricky, you better be believe that politicians formulate *Bait* on a regular basis which they dangle in front of your eyes, gain your interest, then reel you in.

This *Bait* is often presented with the most basic, and scarcest information-just enough to entice. All politicians and lawmakers need is for constituents like you, and I to be moved by what we hear, and once they gain sufficient support from us then they can move forward with getting the legislation past.

There is a famous saying; "All That Glitters Is Not Gold." It is a general saying which is derived from a William Shakespeare play (*The Merchant of Venice*), and originates as far back as the 12th century. Still, it holds true today in the area of politics, and the choices we make as voters. Let the words wash over you for a second; "All That Glitters Is

Not Gold." Therefore not every proposed new law, or words out of a politicians' mouth is for your precise benefit, or even what you, and your family needs. Be mindful of the *Bait*! Examine the rhetoric presented. Do your own research, and ask as many questions as you need to. Contact your state representative, and whichever relevant lawmaker within your reach to get whatever answers you need to. Fully understand the "piece of food" that is laid out in front of you, or else pay the price further down the road when new legislation has been put into place that affects your pockets, your home, and your family, and there is nothing that you can do to reverse it.

Let's follow through with the methodology, or thinking behind the *Bait and Switch*. I have shared much about how the *Bait* works. Politicians dangle the very bare essentials to get you pumped up. To get you excited about the potential of what you are about to receive, then once you're on their hook, only then are the specifics of the initial proposal revealed. Within that revelation, only then are the minute details finally uncovered. The details which may be harmful to you, and your family. Small details that were purposely omitted. What also occurs following the *Bait* is that the promised plan of action is now presented with changes. The new information that was previously omitted on purpose, and the unforeseeable changes is what is referred to as the *Switch*.

Now some believe, and debate whole heartedly that change in politics cannot be avoided. Their argument is that bills can be proposed one year but later be affected by economic changes, and other developments within the society. Nonetheless, others are of the opinion that neglecting to communicate the exact ramifications of a specific legislation in order to get it past-at any cost, including withholding key information-is downright political fraud.

10

Regardless of the debate, it happens. *It does happen!* You are *bait*ed to vote without all the nitty gritty facts. Then once the law passes, you discover vital details have been *switch*ed.

Let's use the much talked about Obamacare or Affordable Care Act as an example. The proposed bill sounded magnificent. It offered health care for all. Under this venture, no one can be denied proper medical service. Obamacare reached far, and wide. It reached across class, age, employment status, and promised benefits to get just about anyone revved up.

Notwithstanding, the little known kicker is that as a result of Obamacare you can get hit with a bill on your taxes. Also, if you record the wrong yearly income, it comes out of your refund before you see it. What is even more interesting is that Doctors are not obligated to accept Obamacare. That is the whole truth, and nothing but the truth. Still this is only a very simple example of the *Bait and Switch* technique conveniently used by lawmakers. It is used in other areas which are not that easily detectable.

Placate

In no way do I assume, or am I trying to infer that you do not know the definitions of these terms. Instead, as a useful tool to illustrate and closely connect how politicians, and lawmakers, strategically use these methods to sway us, or even manipulate us to potentially satisfy their agenda, I would like direct your attention to the definition of the next political control tactic.

According to the Merriam-Webster Dictionary *Placate* is defined as follows:

11

To cause (someone) to feel less angry about something. To soothe or mollify especially by concessions: appease

One such example of lawmakers *placating* the public, was around the Freddie Gray case in Baltimore. In April, 2015, 25 year old Freddie Gray Jr., was arrested by the Baltimore Police Department for what they deemed to be possession of an illegal switchblade. While being transported in a police van, Gray fell into a coma, and was taken to a trauma center. Gray died about 7 days later. His death was attributed to injuries to his spinal cord while in police custody. As a result, six Baltimore police officers associated with his arrest were indicted, and taken into custody.

This incident took place on the heels of other similar deaths of black men while in the custody of police officers, in other states. The Baltimore community responded immediately. They refused to take this sitting down. The residents rioted in the streets, and marched to protest the brutality they, and we-the remainder of the African American population-were convinced was exercised upon Freddie Gray by the six Baltimore police officers. In response when Baltimore's State's Attorney, Marilyn J. Mosby, announced the decision to charge the six officers we immediately felt somewhat vindicated. As a community, it felt as though someone finally heard our cries, correct? It could in *no way* absolve the gruesome death of Eric Garner in New York City, or the shooting of Michael Brown in Ferguson, Missouri but hope was wafting in the air...right?

Nonetheless, let's take a closer look at the Baltimore events. Following Freddie Gray's death-as I made light reference to previously-the streets of Baltimore was run over to with fed-up-ain't-going-to-take-it no-more citizens. Businesses

12

were looted, and burned, and various groups from various corners of the country showed up to march till some sort of change was evident. What were lawmakers to do? Another Ferguson type of long and dirty unrest, times-two, could have been the result. Therefore the Baltimore State Attorney stood boldly. She stood strong, and unwavering. She told us that the matter will be handled, and where justice will prevail. The only thing that never truly came to light was that the six police officers who were charged, were released on lesser bail than the man who died, Mr. Freddie Gray Jr. While we may feel justified that we got what we wanted, if we look closer we will realize that this announcement was made in order to *placate* the community. Otherwise, shouldn't the punishment adequately fit the crime? How is it that these aggressors are allowed to walk out of jail with what seemed like a slap on the wrist, in comparison to the what Freddie Gray experienced? Seems we've been *placated...soothed...appeased.*

The next term was birth close to home---in our neighborhoods, and comes straight out of our very own vernacular. As a result, let's visit the Urban Dictionary for it's definition.

Trickology:
The study of the tricking phenomena with reference of origin, growth, reproduction, structure, and behavior of those imposing a trick and those on the receiving end of a trick.
Or
Trickological phenomena of an organism or a group of organisms performing tricks.

Pretty deep, right? Well as you, and I both know, all these big words explain is that organizations, groups, etc.

perform tricks to simply get over on others, and the method used is trickery, or deception.

What is more important is that people in power, sitting in their high offices, use this to direct the way that you, and I vote. This strategy is also used by big business to get into our pockets. *Trickology* is applied to convince us to buy one way, or another, all the time. If you've missed it, don't feel guilty. It has been in play for decades, and exercised quite expertly. Like magic. It is the method of telling you that you're going to get one thing, but instead you actually get something else. Here's one quick example. Acquiring a foreclosed home, that is actually valued at $500,000 or more, for one dollar ($1) sounds like the dream...doesn't it? At first glance, it sure does to me. If I didn't even know better, I'd be all over it from the jump. Let's do it! Well, have you considered the property taxes that accompanies that? Those costs alone can sink you so far, and in such a way that defeats the purpose of obtaining that item for $1.00. Don't be *tricked*!

Not only does our vote matter, but I can't stress enough the importance-it is CRITICAL-of also understanding what each proposed bill, or law truly means for you, your family, and your community. From matters that affect your finances, your taxes, and laws that can impact your neighborhood, and the structure of the family. I will talk more about this further into the book, but quick question? Do you know that there are current laws that are directly related to the breakdown of the African American family on the books? We will delve further, later on in our conversation, so stay with me.

Some attempts have been made to chip away at changing these laws but the statistics remain outrageous concerning how many of our fathers-African American males-are

14

incarcerated with unnecessary lengthy sentences which don't fit the crime. As a result, they are strategically kept away from leading their homes, thus the breakdown of the culture as a whole. Let's vote...let's fight with the vote that will directly change the law to bring our men home.

Please know that I am talking to you about this from experience. I am a Black male who was once incarcerated myself. To that end, I see the full picture-from both sides. After wising up to what the real game is out here, I can assure you that our voice is loudest, our influence is the greatest, and *change* comes...*change* will take place...*change happens* when we vote, but vote knowledgeable of all the nitty gritty facts that matter.

It's Simple! If you don't like what you're seeing happen to your pocket book, or wallet, your family, your neighborhood, your region, your country; then change the laws - Vote!

****

CHAPTER 3

The Problems That Affect The Inner City

Although our community-the African American (or Black) Community-is scattered throughout various neighborhoods, let's be real. A significant number of our brothers, and sisters still very much reside in the inner city. It's not a secret; neither does it require elaborate statistics right here to explain what life is like, both economically and socially, for individuals who live in the inner city.

For some of us, we once lived there as well. We worked hard, were motivated by others, or our own drive led us to be a part of a different locale. Still, it is advantageous for us to see ourselves as one community...one tribe...one people. *Yes! That's right.* Now, it is not a new notion. I am certain that you have heard it before. Some have even voiced that segregation, in the 60s, was actually a plus for the overall character of our community. Many are of the opinion, including African American scholars, that during that time we rallied around one another with fervor. We looked out for our neighbors, and our neighbors children. Black teachers treated their black students as though they were their own and invested in their overall development and took immense pride in educating them. I am not advocating for returning to that time in history when we were also not all able to freely eat where we wanted to, or shop where we wanted or even earn the way we wanted to. Nonetheless, I must say that it is quite obvious that we are indeed a segregated people. A segregated African-American people today.

You don't believe me?
Okay.
Let's take a second look at the recent unfortunate Freddie Gray Jr., Baltimore episode. What happened in Baltimore has far reaching effects throughout the nation. We have already seen it. The fervency in which people went out to march stemmed from built up frustration about previous disconcerting incidents between police, and our community. Still, the gravity of the situation was a prime opportunity for notable individuals, like celebrities who themselves have risen from the inner city, to speak up. A prime opportunity to let their influence weigh in on the disgraceful events.

Yes. Yes, some popular individuals did show up to march. Celebrated Pro basketball player, Carmelo Anthony returned to his hometown to demonstrate his support. Other well-known folks such as Aaron Maybin, former NFL player, and recording artist Wale were also counted in the number with those who participated to "make some noise" about the shameful event which occurred. Good for them! The passion depicted on their faces, on television, the internet, and print newspapers reflected solidarity. A sense of oneness.

It is actually quite impressive. These individuals identified with, and sensed the pain of *their* own neighborhood. While remarkable there is a tendency, time and again, for us to openly and vigorously represent "our territory" with an intensity not matched for the entire Black community. You see the thing is, unfortunately **tribalism** is alive and well amongst us. When there is a damaging occurrence to the African-American community in New York City, the NYC natives-particularly the famous ones-speak loud, and strong. The same occurs on the west coast, and so on, and so on. We go hard, and are willing to die for our own turf. Gang members of the same ancestry, and skin color will do anything for a member on their turf, but will immediately take out another (of same ancestry, and skin color) from another turf over something trivial. Now I know that the specific gang reference is not a blanket, even stereotypical illustration of Black folks as a whole. Still, there is some likeness to be drawn from it as to how we approach matters as a whole. So please hang in there with me.

If we were to apply the same zeal to protecting, cultivating, and supporting the quality of life, and standard of living of our people as a complete whole-I mean nationwide, beyond "our streets" and beyond our region-we would be further along in many respects. The purpose of this conversation isn't to condemn, criticize nor compare, but it will be helpful for us to note that our Caucasian brothers, and sisters think differently. Much differently. There is no harm in applying what is consistently working well for another group. Like they say, "chew the meat, and spit out the bones." Our Caucasian counterparts regularly look beyond their street, neighborhood or region. Their mindset is broader. When making calculated decisions about who they want in power, they make decisions that will affect generations to come. They make decisions that not only benefit their families, and their little corner of society but the country, domestically and concern themselves with matters internationally.

I can guess what you're thinking, and No! I am in no way discounting that our communities, including the inner city, is in the current state that it is in as a result of the awful past we experienced at the hand of this same group. Nevertheless, it is high time to work smarter, not harder. It is time to be clever, and no longer complain about what is not working, but taking what we have available to us, and making it work for us. We can begin to turn things around for ourselves economically, even politically-and get this-*Nationwide*, if we begin to THINK BIGGER.

THINK BIGGER where your immediate, and diverse neighborhood is concerned as well. The primary intent of this book is to open our eyes. The eyes of my people, the African American people about the *real* and *significant power* that *our vote* has. Yes, that is the goal. However, some of us also live in diverse neighbors, and cities. We share our streets with Hispanics, Asians, whites, Ethiopians etc. To this end, there is a tendency for the **tribalism** mentality to come into play in these instances. We don't see the community fully as ours since it is not completely comprised of all of us. People who look exactly like us, and share the same history. Well, I am here to inform you that while our specific issues are relevant, if you, and you your family share a neighborhood with other ethnic groups, it serves your own purpose well to work cohesively to accomplish whatever goals you would like to realize for your neighborhood.

I am black. I love being black. I love my black family, and my black community. It is out of love for myself, and for all of us that I have grown to appreciate that no group is perfect, and we that can learn something from everyone. I am married. When we began to get to know one another, some of our differences became each other's strengths. We complement one another. God knows that I am not perfect, and she isn't either, but there are things that we offer the other that we each do not possess naturally. In the same way, I believe that we can learn from others. "Chew the meat, and spit out the bones" remember?

Every group has positive traits that we can draw from in order to enhance what we are doing or working to accomplish. We have quite a lot to offer these groups as well. For example, I have learned from my white counterparts that they keep abreast of every move the city is planning for the development of public spaces, as well as for homes. They even know this information ahead of broadcasted announcements. They acquire the right relationships, and leverage them to accomplish what they need, and what they want. This group does not rely on the media to remain informed. They go in search of the details themselves. They carry out personal investigations. They make personal visits to the city officials' offices to uncover any public information that can be uncovered. These individuals remain on top of any taxes that can affect their homes, and their pockets. Then whatever they are unhappy with, they fight back with their vote.

If the white race, or even other ethnic groups, don't like a law they jump in with both feet to initiate change to the law. They will even request that another law be put in place. Our Caucasian brethren take their concerns directly to their state representatives, city officials-whomever necessary-and don't stop chipping away at them until something is done. They are quick to cause a racket. Not the type of racket where buildings are burned, and businesses are thrashed and no lasting change happens. They stir things up by demanding change where it counts. Demanding change where it matters, and that is on the law books. With a change to policy. They are vocal, and outspoken. They are also wise about the avenues they use. It is properly thought out, and strategic. Regardless of who else lives in their neighborhood, they remain diligent. They remain current. They are actively conscientious and do their best to secure the best living experience for themselves, and their family. It is as though they see beyond what is presently happening around them, but instead think ten steps ahead.

In the same way, if you co-exist in a neighborhood with a variety of individuals, it is actually advantageous for your home, and your family to fight for, and protect that neighborhood as a whole. Deciding not to act because it not just "us" inhabiting the community is foolhardy. Living aimlessly, not being aware of the plans for your area is not wise, and can actually hurt you in the long run. Ingest some of the "meat" from your white contemporaries. ***Be proactive, not reactive.*** Unfortunately this is how our community deals with issues. We wait until something detrimental has occurred then act. Act out of anger. Act out of emotion.

I encourage all of us to begin to practice taking the initiative to visit local public offices. Be resourceful. Let's stay abreast of plans for our communities and on top of what is taking place before we are sidetracked. Okay so you may be shouting back, "I don't have time for that, I have to work." Okay. I get it. Work is very important. Not to minimize the importance of your work, or your diligence to provide for your family but there is something much larger at stake here.

If we are to break the cycle of the **Bait** and **Switch**, and **Trickology**, having an adverse effect on our lives, we are going to have to take matters into our own hands. We are going to need to use initiative, pre-thought and planning. Jump in front of the issue, and no longer allow the issue sneak up on you. Additionally, let's open our minds to realize that taking action. That voting on issues that matter to our diverse neighborhoods also matter to our own homes.

Your neighborhood is your neighborhood, regardless of the makeup. It is still yours!

Therefore, do not allow tribalism in which ever form-whether "hood" versus "hood" or your home versus your mixed neighborhood-to be a barrier toward achieving our overall-bigger-goal of exercising our *right to vote*, and in turn growing our political *power*. Growing bigger political muscles.

Envision the status of the country today...
How are you doing with providing for your family?
Are you limited in being able to provide for your family sufficiently?
Does a mistake from your past stand in your way?

How are the current laws preventing you from gaining an income?
Men: Are you truly able to provide for your kids despite past mistakes?
Women: Is your family the unit you desire-where your children's father is present, or is he incarcerated unjustly?
What do you envision for your children, even grandchildren in the coming years?
*What stands in the way of you, and your life being **all** that it can be?*

Granted, the complete answers to these questions don't only reside with the laws that are in place. The make-up of our various families, and any shortcomings don't rest squarely on the shoulders of the "powers-that-be". However, due to us often turning a blind eye and failing to take action where it matters, we don't realize that there are indeed some regulations on the books that can lock us into an unfortunate cycle. When new laws are proposed, we either don't do our part to ensure that they are indeed best for us, or we ignore them all together. Many men are incarcerated way longer than they deserve. Sentences are trumped up. This is not mouth service, it's a *reality*.

New laws have been introduced recently to reduce sentences based on the nature of the crime. Yet, in many areas not enough of us are knowledgeable of this information. In some instances, not many of us appear to really be concerned about this very important issue. While women are also victims of these unfortunate circumstances, a significantly larger number of our men are affected which snowballs into having an overall impact on the family. There is a breakdown in many, many, many of our families, when the father is not present. Some homes have substituted the male presence. That works fine according to the circumstance. However, if a father can be with his children, every effort should be made to help him be with them. This benefits the family, and in the long-run, the Black community overall.

Even economically, it is more cost effective for a man to run one home, with one unit as opposed to managing finances for his residence, and one another...even two. I am not trying to step on any toes. Still, let me say that this goes beyond being a moral situation. It's just makes good sense. It makes good sense for the children who may not feel obligated to respect, and receive discipline from a stranger- or number of strangers. It is a more stable environment, thus discouraging young people from seeking a "father-figure" in all the wrong places, and among the wrong influences. Additionally, to underline the point I raised earlier, this is the best overall financial route.

I mentioned earlier that I was incarcerated in the past. I was indicted on possession charges-true...With the intention to distribute-not true. I am grateful that the sentence was not an insurmountable number of years. I am also grateful that I was able to turn things around. Now married, with a daughter I see the value of my being at home and not sitting in a jail cell. Not able to properly participate in what is going on in own my home. I can imagine my being away from my daughter, and she experiencing a completely different life style. Her mother, seeking any which way to provide for her, giving her a fraction of the time that she is able to give her now, and possibly relying on a male stranger, or two, to improve her circumstances. That is not good enough for me! That shouldn't be good enough for any other father out there.

I said all that to say, the laws targeted at keeping black men away from their families longer than necessary, for petty infractions need to change. When laws are proposed regarding reducing sentences we need to be alert, and educate ourselves. This is the family we are talking about. The heartbeat of the society. Therefore if laws which are currently in place can be changed, laws that affect the heartbeat of our community, we need to grab hold of the information, and examine it. Take a closer look.

Don't be **baited**, and then **switched** up on.

Don't allow yourself to be **placated**.

Don't be **tricked**....

...Instead, for the sake of your household, your family, your community, and the plight of the inner city, be enlightened. For every law proposed, your vote...your voice matters. Even if it is not officially on the ballot, be active and call or visit your representative. Yes, our white contemporaries have a huge head start economically. They were not subjected to slavery, and the after effects that followed. Nevertheless, in 2015, please remember that we have a very important card to play. Let's make full use of the rights that democracy has afforded us. Therefore, again, *let's work smarter instead of harder.* Do you think that Caucasians, sit and take whatever is presented to them? NO! They remain...I said, *remain* conscious---remain knowledgeable about what is really taking place, and they DO NOT sit back and simply accept what is presented to them, if it does not fit within the scheme they have for their households, and overall community. Petitions, phone calls, lobbies, and the like are put into play immediately.

Your white neighbors, and white co-workers don't rest fully on their "white privilege" to progress. They remain conscious. They remain active.

Jobs

Pardon me. This subject is close to home. I am a man with a record, who has successfully acquired a college degree, then have been afforded the opportunity to be in some very influential circles. Still, I don't take it lightly that it is a daily struggle to properly provide for my family. Higher education, or not, being stained with a record can be an obstacle to every hustle. Technically, with a criminal record you can prevented from getting a job as basic as a position as a trash man. When I couldn't secure employment I used my initiative and became an employer myself. I turned my obstacle into an opportunity. There isn't anything on the legal books that prohibits that. There is no prevention to becoming an enterprise. I started a Temp Agency where I gathered individuals with specific skills and assigned them where needed.

It is also important to note that our right to vote touches every area of our lives. It is essential to know the laws that can stand in your way, even against your plans to succeed at a good job that pays a good wage. Additionally, planning a trip to college for your children or yourself? The military promotes that they can be helpful with that. However, it is imperative to first accurately investigate what is the full scope of those requirements before going that route. It is not all that it is cracked up to be. Believe me! I also enlisted. Search "behind-the-veil" and know what you are signing up for, as a whole. Sure, the government wants to add to its defense team, but before you commit under the guise of getting college paid for, enter into the decision fully alert. Do not allow the *Bait*, and *Switch* to leave you in a predicament that you had not anticipated.

I talk about this elsewhere as well but student loans are another aspect to acquiring a higher education. I fully support attaining a Bachelor's degree, even a Master's

Degree. It has become more, and more of a necessity to have that credential attached to your name. It does not guarantee higher paid work but it is certainly helpful toward acquiring it. My only word of caution would be to, again, do the due diligence to understand precisely what is at stake when taking on a government student loan. Is this your only option? What are the specifics of the loan? Where is there an opportunity to demand that this also be an issue that is included on the ballot for a vote? Of course President Obama is aware of the tight noose that student loans can be around our necks. His proposals to dismiss them are thoughtful. Nevertheless it is not enough. It does not apply to government issued ones. Think about it for a brief moment. We apply for loans to get a higher education that will lead to a higher paid job, in order to make investments, like a home down the road. However, if we are unable to repay our loans, our credit score suffers, and we are left unable to secure the investment we once made plans for. We must be diligent, and action minded for own ourselves. As a people across the country, and in our local areas, where are the statues or regulations that prevent us from bettering ourselves so that we can increase our income without being dead broke in the long run. Individually, as well as together, let's educate ourselves, and drive the point home that we want change and take the actual physical steps to achieve it for our own sake, and the sake of our children.

I keep moving forward. I press. I push. I am an entrepreneur who gathers all the facts in every circumstance, and builds upon what I learn. It is not easy, but I have a goal, and a determination to sufficiently cover my family. They will NOT be left hanging under my watch. Coupled with my life experiences, my Administration of Justice degree has supplied me with much insight into what is really going on. I fought to attain my Bachelor's degree.

Still at that level I was not a good reader. Nonetheless with the help of one professor, who recognized it, I persevered because I instinctively knew that despite being a former convict there was more to gain from life. I wanted to be smart about life this time around. Being locked in a jail cell like a caged animal is not for me. Particularly with the beautiful family that I now have. I observed successful individuals, as well as those in leadership for some time. I now have a clear view of who are the puppets, the puppeteers, and what are the puppet strings.

Let's work to cut those puppet strings. With the clear view that I have. With each obstacle that I have had to work around, or bulldoze, I am here to encourage you to know a little more, to be enlightened. Let's turn this thing around. Do you know someone who has been locked up for a drug charge, and is held to a sentence not fitting the crime, and they can't get home to their family? In early 2015, President Barack Obama shortened the sentences of 22 drug convicts, including 8 serving life sentences. His goal is to begin reducing harsh sentences, delivered under outdated guidelines. The President's hopes is to make the judicial system fairer. This makes sense, right? Lots of sense!

In six years, President Obama has approved a total of 43 commutations. There may be more by the end of his "reign". Still, no one is going to fight for something like this, like we can. If we are not hot on the heels of our representatives, or staying abreast of laws that are proposed. Laws that are important to us, and that "haters" want off-the-table. Or if we're not actively voting for the ones that we can, then who will look out for us like we can? Who?

Returning to commutating sentences. It is hard enough to get work due to the current job market, let alone trying to provide for your family tied to a sentence, or having a blemished record. Therefore, when there is opposition to pass laws that will improve a man's status and enable him to adequately provide for his family as well as establish an inheritance-like other communities always wisely do-then it is critical that you throw your hat in the ring.

If you think that I am repeating myself here. Yes I am. Like my military training thought me, we got to hear it, and repeat it often, in order to get it good. That is partly how I summed up the process then, and it remains true today. I am eager for you to "get it good". I am eager for my fellow African-Americans to realize the full picture. To visualize the entire "the system" that we have failed to maximize. Pardon me but our white counterparts maximize "the system" so well that they are able to keep us somewhat trapped just because we do not. I must stress the importance of knowing what is occurring around us-and to us. Gather the details. When laws are proposed regarding your neighborhood, what are the far reaching effects? Will it be beneficial to your environment in the short-term alone? How will your home, neighborhood, community be affected in the long run? Take action through voting, and actively making your voice...actually insisting that your voice be heard. Here's the thing. Do you know that if we refuse to accept whatever is dished out, and take a stand through the means that truly gets the attention of "the man"-his precious constitutional laws-then "he" has no choice but to pay attention. But to sit up, and listen.

Beyond turning around those instances where a criminal record restricts employment, and its impact on the inner city, these locations have also been targeted with pointed tactics to hinder the vote. It has been documented that our neighborhoods-Yes, black neighborhoods-have been directly contacted to throw us off the scent of the actual

28

location of polling stations, by those who are clearly threatened by the way they believe our vote will be cast. Folks were being called, and given flyers, in Nashville, to the incorrect places to vote.

What? You say ask.

Yes! True story.

Hello! Wake all the way up my beautiful brothers and sisters.

Clearly our vote does matter! We have the power to turn the tide. Gather the details. Know the far reaching extent of your vote. Not just how it will impact the community today, or tomorrow, but in the years to come.

Consider: What are you trying to accomplish with your vote?

It's like this: You're waving around a $100 bill in front of your child. He or she asks you for either candy, a pair of shoes or a bicycle. Which item would benefit them the most in the long term? Which one will serve them best? Beyond making them hyper, candy will pass straight the body. Shoes, depending on how they are cared for, will provide a limited number of wears. The bicycle is durable. It also serves various functions, and depending on the age of the child, can help you out too. It doubles as an errands vehicle. You be the judge. Thoroughly weigh---thoroughly examine your vote.

Investment

The Merriam-Webster dictionary defines *Investment* as:
The outlay of money usually for income or profit: capital outlay; also.
While this definition focuses on the investment of money, or capital, I would also like to add that the way in which we vote is an investment. Don't get me wrong. I am all for investment in the traditional sense as well. Nonetheless what I would like to point out is, as a community, as a

people, it is to our benefit that we participate in both monetary investment, *and* the profit we gain from voting intelligently.

In Camden, NJ the citizens chose to vote to keep crime low in the area by increasing police presence. Sounds fantastic, right? I mean looking in from the outside, what is better than being able to rely on this kind of official protection? Well, what they didn't examine was that in voting to increase police presence they lost a significant amount of their most productive residents.

18-35 year olds are usually the object of police attention. Naturally this sector of the Camden population felt like they were being harassed, and began disappearing one by one. In addition to that, with a heavy police presence, businesses become adversely affected. Customers assume that the location is unsafe and don't want to purchase products there.

What this teaches us is that heavier police presence does not equal progress. Instead it serves to devalue the community, and hurt it in ways outside of just protection. I'll share another story with you. Again in Camden. It's a violation to loiter in a drug zone. Two gentlemen. Two white gentlemen sat near the bus station, playing chess. The police arrested them for hanging out in the drug zone. As a result of all of this increased police presence, current businesses are gradually folding up. Potential businesses are deterred from developing in this area. Individuals are discouraged, and find it a hassle to visit family members in the neighborhood. All of this is as a result of how a vote went down, during an election. Residents voted for what they considered to be a healthy option for their neighborhood. In the long run, it is doing damage instead.

Therefore, it is important-down right critical-to understand your vote from all sides. Take a 360 degree view before you make a decision. Get to know, the return on your vote. How does your vote, and what you vote for truly profit you, your family, your neighborhood, state, region, and country? *Get to know it! Do the research. Dig deep, and examine its long term reach.*

Another example can be found in the Willingboro township of New Jersey. Homes are deteriorating as a result of the way residents voted, not realizing that one "harmless" vote compounded in to lowering the property value. All in all, your vote can help or hinder your investment. Your investment in your home, a business, and on a larger scale, your investment in your family.

If you want to see change, don't sit and "take it"! Don't just accept what is presented to you. Look closer. Dig deeper. If it is affecting your money, and the ability to properly provide for your family, and future generations at large, don't settle for it! Take a page out of 'their book': Fight back with your VOTE---with your intelligently researched VOTE!

****

CHAPTER 4

Law makers are moved by VOTES. They are moved by who votes, and the number of votes. You will be taken seriously when you VOTE!

The Root of the Problems...

The root cause. The issue that has led me to...that has stirred me up to sit down and write this book is the simple fact that we don't vote. As a whole, we are lackluster. We lack motivation, even the inspiration and fail to fully understand, on multiple levels, how we can steer our quality of life with our vote.

Earlier on I indicated that the United States is unique in that we are privileged to be able to vote on several levels. We are afforded the ability to vote on the city level, the state level, and on the national level. In many, many, many countries they generally only have a say in who runs the country. Yet with all this wonderful privilege, even entitlement, we still do not realize the power in our grasp. We still do not realize what we have in our hands.

Each vote can shape our neighborhoods, when we intelligently identify the right persons to vote for. A vote can reduce the value of our homes, *or* increase it. A vote can enhance our children's education, or leave it lacking. The right vote can grow your business, and/or your neighbor's business or repel profits. There may not be a specific issue on the ballot that directly correlates to one of, or is similar to, the above mentioned topics but there will be someone on the ballot with similar values, or who mirrors your mindset. This is the sort of person you can vote for to push your agenda through. We can strategically and wisely investigate to discover a candidate, a council person, and the like whose platform matches your purposes. Yes!

To get to the nitty gritty, many of us plainly are not as invested in our community as we should be. Unfortunately, we still rely on the media for information instead of learning the "real deal" for ourselves. You remember the following terms, **Bait** and **Switch**, **Placate**, and ***"Trickology"***? Well, it is very easy to release to the electronic, and print media whatever information "they" want you to know. It is up to us to sift through the information, look behind the smoke screen, truly understand the ramifications, and the ins and outs.

Again, it is critical that we KNOW WHAT we are voting for. It is of absolute importance that we understand what politicians are up to. When a law is proposed, or a topic comes up for debate, go behind the curtain, if you will. Also, become acutely knowledgeable and understand how the current laws are affecting you. Furthermore KNOW WHO you are voting for. Become closely familiar with their track record, and with their background. Have they been consistent, or have they swayed with the tide, brought on by negative peer pressure or impending stardom? Have they done all within their power to deliver on their promises?

For example, in relation to the true story I shared in Chapter 3, about increased police presence in Camden, New Jersey-that specific issue was not on the ballot. However the residents elected the mayoral candidate with the mindset, and/or agenda which led to that outcome. That is what made the difference. In another example, Philadelphia is working to make it law that the state have a record of every home which possesses a security camera posted at the front. This will enable them to secure the camera footage if a crime should take place in that neighborhood. Would you want this for your area? Would you want to be known for turning over evidence of a crime that happened right in front of your home? Suppose the burglar gets wind of that news? Would you want that to be a law, where you didn't have a choice in the matter? Would you welcome that requirement?

Hence the importance to fully KNOW WHO, and KNOW WHAT a candidate-even at the lowest level-is really...truly...totally all about. You can vote a person into position, and vote some crazy stuff into place as a result.

Lack of Voting...

Beyond what I perceive as the real issues why African Americans seem to need a push, even an incentive to vote, I would like *you* to take some time to also chew on it. *What do you believe deters us from becoming truly invested in the electoral process?* Since our ancestors have put their lives on the line, being mulled over by dogs, prodded by law enforcement, and beaten bloody in the sixties there hasn't seem to be any true self-motivation among us as a people. What do you think keeps us-as a group-from doing *all* that we can to fight back with *the vote.*

Of course there are some legitimate reasons why we don't make it to the polls. Many of us are juggling more than one shift just to provide for our families. To that end, I declare that any, and every Election Day should be an official holiday. Granted federal type jobs do allow for about two hours to vote. Still, the time it takes to commute to the polls, and stand in line is two hours alone. What about the neighbor, brother or cousin who doesn't have a government type job? Moving shifts around, or getting paid leave is almost out of the question for some other jobs.

That is not good enough! Something needs to be done about the time allotted to vote regardless of the occupation. That is a law change that I can certainly get behind. For those of us eager to vote and participate in our rights, there

34

shouldn't be any barriers. For the single mother working at McDonalds, *there shouldn't be any barriers*. For the construction worker desperate to provide for his family, *there shouldn't be any barriers*. For the Nanny holding things down while her wealthy employers cast their vote, *there shouldn't be any barriers*...and so on, and so on. Any, and every Election Day should be a full free day for any, and everyone to cast their vote.

Not Knowing All Your Rights...

Our right to vote is our just claim or title to the democratic process. The Voting Rights Act of 1965 opened the door for us to forego all the previous bull crap, in order to participate fully in this here United State of America. In spite of our history, and regardless of the injustices that we still experience, the general society refuses to face up to the onslaught of white-privilege, and our history of economic imbalance etc. Nevertheless, we now have an in. Since 1965, if we should approach it cunningly and strategically. We can grab a *firm* hold of the opportunity to make use of this **Right**, and take control of our lives, our neighborhoods, our communities, and the outcome for generation to come.

Still we have hurdles to overcome. I speak from the vantage point of having a criminal record. Once upon a time I was stopped by police with drugs on me. The intent to distribute was also pinned on me, although it was far from the truth. Nonetheless I have this blemish, and it goes with me wherever I go. It hangs over me wherever I put my hand to do something productive. At every turn when I'm trying to provide for my family, I am reminded. I also had to take it into consideration when voting. I believe in this thing wholeheartedly. I am not writing this book because I felt like stringing some sentences together. Just to make empty noise. This is not an   attempt to make a name for myself.

I am from the inner city. I have been incarcerated. I am a Black man. I have seen the worse. I have experienced the worse. I am quite familiar with unfair treatment. I have witnessed the whole story, from the inside out. From the front, and the back. I have served in the military. I have studied. I am a family man. I understand. I know the totality of what we confront on a daily basis extremely well. I'm not trying to suggest that I have suffered more than my brother, or my sister, but I do have a front row seat to the realities of the system.

In addition to facing those realities, I have slithered behind-the-curtain-so to speak. I have personally dug deep. I have had the opportunity to associate with some of the power brokers. I am not too proud, and refuse to be too narrow minded, to learn from those who are using the system to their benefit. As a result, since I have been armed with the knowledge that making a dent in the laws is the way to have some control of, well at least of my own life, I certainly practice what I preach.

As a former offender of the law, I have had to investigate all my rights to be able to effectively cast my vote. Check this out. According to the Democracy Restoration Act 2015, introduced by Representative John Conyers (D-Mich) in March 2015, only Vermont and Maine do not restrict current or former inmates from voting. Thirty-five states restrict former inmates on parole from voting. Thirty-one ban those on felony probation, and 11 states command lifetime voting bans in some cases, according to the bill.

Thanks to Lydia O'Connor of the Huffington Post, we learn that close to 6 million Americans are unable to vote due to their criminal history. Wow! Terribly large number, right? As you probably suspect, the majority of that number are African Americans. I don't know about you, but just viewing those figures I am taken aback. Even though I am included in that number, it is indeed overwhelming to envision.

The Voting Rights Act of 1965 allowed us to overcome one hurdle, but we are faced with yet another one. It is no secret that prisons are overpopulated with members of our community. This unfortunate circumstance further disables us from taking the full control of our homes, within the rights that have been afforded us. Some of you-just a few- may be thinking, "Well, if you do the crime, then you got to do the time." The thing is, although that statement is suitably justified, many of our brothers (and sisters) are serving much longer sentences than they deserve.
John Conyers should be commended for introducing the bill to restore voting rights to ex-felons. Unfortunately many former convicts are not confident, and are even confused, about their own voting rights. Among many others, this is one significant reason why I am talking to you today. If you are an ex-convict, like myself, you can regain control of your life, your home, and your family. If incarceration is not a part of your past do you have a family member, or friend, who has a criminal record? Do they shy away from the voting polls because they don't fully know their rights? Go tell them. Give them a call. Knock on their door. Tell them that you know a man named Eric Scott who has been on both sides of the system, and can inform them first hand that a shady past does not prevent them from securing the full future they dream of for themselves, and their family.

I am not saying that it will be a simple reset. I am not saying that it will be a quick turnaround but what I am saying is that with initiative, effort, and some self-education it is possible to move forward, and build something meaningfully successful. Your intelligent vote is one step toward reaching that end. Be mindful, like I said before, it will not be a cake walk but it is doable. I am not going to pretend that I do not run in to obstacles time, and time again.

Working within my own limitations, as a result of my history, I always have to think outside the box. Every time I try to start a business, I am confronted with various road blocks. Of course there is competition from similar businesses, but either my criminal past is an issue or there are dozens of hurdles to leap over to get a profitable enterprise off the ground. I attempted to open my own waste management business. My establishment would be tasked with visiting apartments, and alleviating residents of having to trek to the apartment compound dumpsters. Within the time frame that I was going through the process of being railroaded with fee, after fee, ample red tape, and regulation, after regulation a larger company formed, and swooped in to cover my market.

The large costs of fees, and mile long red tape is enough to dissuade anyone from becoming an entrepreneur, particularly with other individuals who are able to secure large capital, and who have friends in "high places" looking out for them. Let alone having to disclose your criminal past. It can be daunting. The thing is, many of the laws regarding small businesses should not be there. Furthermore, these laws may not specifically be on the ballot, but voting for the right person with the right mindset can certainly make the difference.

Think about the businesses you, or a family member, has tried to start. Several regulations on the books have worked against you to prevent it in several instances, not so? The next step is to familiarize yourself with the laws. Acquire the information. Request change from your representatives, and vote to demand change. I have not stopped. I continue to research opportunities to build something for my family. Something that will be long standing. Provision that will supply them with higher education, and a full life-even long after I have left this earth.

I am grateful to be able to provide for my daughter, son, and wife these days, without living pay check to pay check. Being intelligent about investment is quite advantageous also. Conducting research to learn the best way to invest-whether property or elsewhere-is key. If it is property, this is where your vote comes in. The laws from state to state vary but if we do not know what we are getting into, we can be *Tricked* into accepting a bill of goods. Often time taxes are hidden, and creep up on us at the very last minute. Particularly during the sale of a home.
I recall a friend who was preparing to sell his home. Gentrification is infiltrating many north east cities. I warned him that he stood to lose money if he sold his house. A significant portion would be absorbed by various categories of taxes, and his profit would be minimal, if any. After my friend gathered all the facts, he thought through the situation carefully and he decided to hold on to his home.

Many laws are not widely known but neatly tucked away while law makers, and politicians only reveal part of the story in order to give us the usual *Bait*, and *Switch.* Again, we can expose the whole plan. Through familiarizing ourselves. Through asking the right questions. Through getting to the core, and holding our representatives, and other law makers accountable, then making an educated vote we can beat them at their own game.

Your VOTE actually makes a difference to your day to day quality of life. Voting allows more control of your life, your neighborhood, your community. Your VOTE affects every area of your life.

****

CHAPTER 5

The Effects of the Problem

Being sent away to prison for too long...

The Merriam-Webster dictionary defines the word *Problem* partly as:
> *Difficulty in understanding something.*

In Chapter 4 I entered into a discourse about the **Root of the Problem**. I broke it into **Lack of Voting**, and **Not Knowing All Your Rights**. Now I would like to offer that these root causes can be summed up by "difficulty in understanding..." Not understanding that we do indeed have leverage, that we have "a gun in the gun fight". I don't truly believe we understand that we possess the power that we do. We have been trained, subconsciously, to *understand* what we currently do *understand*.

For some of us, we are aware of our voting power. Some of us *do understand* the full range of our rights. Some of us *do* make full use of the democratic process. Some of us *do* grasp the broad scope of the privilege we possess, in comparison to citizens of other countries. However, the number is not sufficient, quite yet. The number is not enough to make the sort of in roads necessary to impact our culture within the larger culture, significantly.

When it is no longer reported that African-Americas have the overall low level of credit that we currently do, then we know that we are heading somewhere. When ownership is a priority-and not just homes-then we know we are heading somewhere.

The only way to get to where we need to be. The only way to somewhat attain to that level playing field is to change the laws, and begin to even things out at the polls. Until we grasp that in its fullness. Until we grasp that as a whole. *Until we understand*, then the effects of the problem will be *NO Change*.

NO change to long prison sentences. NO change to small business regulations which serve to hinder, instead of help us gain economic independence. NO change to ridiculous, and hidden taxes-in property, and otherwise. Laws, and regulations will continue to be forced upon us like a prison sentence. Ironic? No? In no way is it my intention to be scandalous, or condescending but I would like to submit that we allow ourselves to be subjected to a form of slavery when we do not fully live within the rights that we have been afforded.

Some of your responses may be that, "I do vote!" That is remarkable! Congratulations. I truly mean that! However, I have a follow-up question. "How do you vote?" Do you understand the full ramifications of your decision? Earlier I mentioned a vote by residents in the Willingboro township of New Jersey which resulted in the neighborhood deteriorating. What was a seemingly harmless, and even beneficial choice compounded in the neighborhood depreciating over a number of years. At the ballot, residents were asked to decide about a simple policy change to the front of the homes in the area. Seemingly this change would be beneficial. The outcome would appear to improve the neighborhood overall. Unfortunately voters did not investigate. They didn't dig deeper to analyze what a slight change to the way in parking at your home can snowball in defacing the neighborhood.

Instead there was a trickle down-and by down, I mean downhill-effect. As a result, one by one the neighborhood emptied. What will it take to revive this community? In my humble opinion, I believe that the right vote. The right well researched, and fully enlightened vote, with the right candidate to match, can turn things around.

I encourage you, that it is time to break the cycle. Here is the knowledge right here, right now, and you have the means to break the cycle. Let's largely narrow the instances where we are regularly **Baited**, only to get *the* **Switch**. We need not be distracted by what is fed in order to **Placate** us. Don't get stuck in a never ending loop. With this information, you can realize every instance where there is an attempt to **Trick** you.

Do you want to see prison sentences reduced? - Break the Cycle, Vote!
Do you want to see Black small businesses grow? - Break the Cycle, Vote!
Do you want to see our neighborhoods develop attractively? - Break the Cycle, Vote!
Do you want to see unnecessary taxes on our homes etc. dissipate? - Break the Cycle, Vote!

Although well known today, the issue of long prison sentences is not sufficiently addressed with the urgency it deserves. This topic is a significant factor capable of contributing to the demise of the African American community. Despite the efforts put forward by President Barack Obama and his government, we-the people who this impacts the greatest-ought to actively participate in reducing long prison sentences. We need to bring our brothers, and our sisters home. We have the ability to contribute to breaking the cycle of broken homes, and broken families.

Families are the foundation on which strong societies are built upon. Our society-our own community-is being specifically, and dangerously harmed by these long prison sentences, and the longer we turn a blind eye to the reality of this epidemic the further fragmented we become, and can completely lose our footing.

If together, we ALL refuse to "take-it", and become a mobilized force through our VOTE, this sort of demonstration of solidarity will not be able to be ignored. It will not be able to be refused!

Play Victim?...

The other alternative is to do the very minimum, and watch the cycle replay. To sit back and watch it spin seamlessly out of control as the same tactics are played out by politicians, and we are subjected to be on a disadvantaged footing for a never ending period of time.

It is easy to blame "the man" or another ethnic group for the current status of the circumstances we face in our neighborhoods, at our children's schools, with acquiring consistent health care, housing and so on. It may even be justified. Yet right now, today, we possess all the rights, and have been presented with the privilege, as a people, to take responsibility for the advancement of our own people. May I remind you that in the midst of our awful past, our forefathers refused to accept their plight, and furiously fought to escape it. SO although in these modern times, we are not enslaved on the cotton field, if we are not more proactive, we can find ourselves trapped in a cycle cunningly devised for us to remain disadvantaged.

Again, what is the alternative? What are your plans for securing a bountiful future for your family line? It's not about me. It's not just about you. The **Bait**, and **Switch**. The strategy of **Placating**. The **"Trickology"**. None of this will end after we have moved on. After we have entered the grave. Granted, politicians do not solely exercise these strategies toward Black people. Still, we are significantly setback with our overall progress as a result. We have taken several steps forward, yet we get pulled back a few more when laws-both which have been previously instituted, and within our life time-are not challenged effectively.

It is *very* important that we come together. This is not some empty speech from a lofty politician. I have no agenda. I have nothing to gain except to see my own people wake up, and use the tools handed them through voting intelligently. I cannot say it enough that being united in our approach to challenge the laws, policies, and regulations will create an impact. The more united we are at the polls, the larger the voice. The larger the voice, the more noise we make. Remember, if everyone refuses to accept "IT"...if everyone decides to remain on top of the issues, and be active as a people, with our vote, we will make waves. We will interrupt the status quo. We will begin to show our hand of real power.

If you don't like the rules that you are dictated to you, don't play the victim. Let's change it through our VOTE!

****

CHAPTER 6

The Power Of The Vote

It would appear that the basis of all that we are discussing is *power*. There are those who believe that they indeed possess power through the nature of their supremely high positions, and not to mention as a result of their wealthy friends who fund their prominent status. It seems as though they carry out their agendas to bolster their way of life, and the way of life of those like them.

Very little, or genuine thought is given to how another group, operating from an unleveled playing field, can work upwards to reach that same level without encountering endless manufactured obstacles. Are we not operating from a different place than those who manage government? For 400 years wealth was multiplied for "them" as a result of the toil, and sweat of our ancestors, and we have not seen *ANY* of it! Absolutely NOTHING!

When restitution was offered in the form of 40 acres, and a mule following the American Civil War, there was no delivery on the promise. Talk about hope dashed! If we possessed the privilege to mobilize and vote then, like we do today, can you imagine where we would be had that been an issue on the ballot? Can you imagine where we'd be financially if we stood together, and handled things with the power of the vote-even back then?

Let's take some time to break down the word *Mobilize*.
Note that the first three letters of the word is MOB.
The Merriam-Webster dictionary defines *Mobilize* as:
: to bring (people) together for action
: to come together for action
: to make (soldiers, an army, etc.) ready for war

It also describes *Mob* as*:*
: a large group or crowd of people who are angry or violent or difficult to control
: a large number of people

We are a group. We are quite significant in number. We can be a *Mob*. We can be a passionate *Mob* who intelligently comes together for action. We don't need to use violence. Oh no! Violence will only give "them" an excuse to imprison us unjustly, and for inordinate lengths of time. Instead come together in strength. Let's roll deep with the fighting power we possess.

You see the vote supplies us with power since challenging the laws, and policies with the democratic process hits "them" right where it counts. It is the only language that lawmakers understand emphatically.

There is *Power* in Your *Vote* to affect *Jobs*.
There is *Power* in Your *Vote* to affect *Investment*.
There is *Power* in Your *Vote* to affect your *Family*.

I know we all know the definition of the word Power. I also know that we all secretly desire power in some form or fashion. Yet, I have found that we often struggle to realize the Power that we have with regards to our Vote. If we truly did. If we fully understood the far reaching depths of

the power we hold when we cast our vote knowing all the facts, and all the ramifications.
We will certainly cause the policy makers to sit upright and pay attention.

Where can we get government to create job opportunities with our vote? How can we impress upon them, our requirement to supply the accurate wage for the task performed? How can we prevent industry from increasingly taking jobs outside of the United States? It is with our vote. It may not be a direct or specific vote. It may be indirect, by voting in the right person for the job who possesses similar ideals to you. Can you imagine what can be accomplished if we took the time to become involved with identifying the most appropriate candidate through productive investigation? Can you imagine how the political pot will be stirred when an educated *Mob* gets behind the right person to accomplish what we need-truly need-for our neighborhoods, and for our families?

Can you imagine the sort of political mindset which instead of rent assistance allows our community to invest in property by supplying the abandoned, or foreclosed homes at an extremely minimal cost? These homes will be revived, and more African Americans will become home owners. Don't you know someone living in a cramped space? Someone trying to be comfortable, with their sizable family, in a small apartment? Someone who would appreciate, value, and take great care of their own home, but can't afford it?

Whether it is someone else, or yourself, you deserve---*we deserve*---to make our vote count! I cannot say it enough, and I will say it as much as I need to. There is Power at the polls. There is Power in our vote. Lawmakers, and politicians take note of protests, and marches. They even take note of riots but they really, and truly sit up straight and *pay full attention* when the numbers at the voting booths are substantial. They *truly listen* when they realize the outcome of our vote. Voting intelligently, once we understand the outcome, not just today, but for the long term speaks volumes. Very, very loud volumes. We are considered a force to be reckoned.

When we vote in the numbers that we should, and in the wise manner we ought, we will begin to see changes in our communities, and in our own lives personally. This enlightenment, that we have significant power in causing change to laws, will bolster our overall confidence. It will trigger a domino effect where we begin to become even more interested, and invested in what is taking place in Washington, D.C., and in our own City Councils. Politicians will even need to think twice about executing their **Bait**, and **Switch**, **Placating**, and **Trickology** tactics.

Look, you are able to shake things up. You have got the *Power*. You have the *Power* to challenge local, to national politicians when they make a proposal. Now remember, not everything that sounds good on the onset is necessarily for your best. Lawmakers talk a good talk until they hook you, then the entire script can be flipped or the "small print" in the actual law may be damaging. So, let me encourage you once more to hold them to the fire. Dig deeper. Fully understand the proposal from all sides, and know how it will affect your life for the long haul.
Therefore, ask as many questions as you want. Contact your representative as much as you like, but use your right, your privilege, your *Power*, your *Vote* to take good care of yourselves, your family, and your homes.

Your investments are affected by your vote. Taxes on your homes, and home sales. Trifling regulations to stall small business growth. Where are your investments being touched adversely?

Where have you sniffed out injustices that are costing you big time? Well, take it directly to the lawmakers. Demand change. Identify the candidate who is like minded, and consistent. Then turn things around in the booth. The voting booth.

Guess what?
We have the Power!
We possess the influence.
We have the ability to turn things.
We have the capability to cause change.
It is in our numbers. It is in our force.
We are a Voting MOB!

****

CHAPTER 7

The Power of Not Letting People Vote

The powers that be do realize the sort of power that we possess. That is why they pull out all their tricks including telling us what we want to hear. They understand that if we come together in the way that we ought to, that we are a force, and have a voice that can be detrimental to their agenda. They have seen what is possible at those times when we are driven, and organized. It was evident prior to the 2012 election. The opposition tried to bar African Americans, who they may have deemed less enlightened, or knowledgeable, from being able to vote by any means necessary. From squabbles over an identification card to hindering party volunteers. They know. They know just how much of an impact we can have if we ban together. Hence, digging up any small issue to stall or prevent the power that we can have at the polls.

Well, this is dangerous territory. Not enabling citizens to exercise their right is downright nasty, and risky. It can lead to civil disobedience. It will result in forcing individuals to comply with rules they were not able to participate in making, later down the road. Now, does that make any sense? Still, lawmakers try to get away with it. If we are to present a united front as a people, all of us...ALL...must be able to vote. *Let's be reminded that Lawmakers know the Power of the vote.* They know the Power of a group that is MOBilized. Therefore, as sad as the reality sounds, they work hard to cook up ways to block us from voting.

Blockades such as instituting the Voter Photo ID laws. Some of you may think, "What's wrong with that? "Voting is a the right of citizens. Therefore, folks simply need to prove they are citizens." Or something like that. Right? I hear you. This is a legitimate statement. It is a valid opinion, but please know that for many Americans who have been living, working, and paying taxes. For those who have contributed to the overall economic growth of the society for many years, that obtaining a photo ID card may not be that simple. There are senior citizens who are unable to get around. They are not able to secure the help to assist them with the regular upkeep of such matters as a new identification card. Some are financially challenged, or have complications in their past that make updating their IDs somewhat similar to going through a maze with no end in sight. Red tape multiplied by red tape, multiplied by red tape mounds up like a bullet proof vest. Our seniors who helped blaze the trail for us to have this right in the first place, are often barred from voting as a result of one detail that can be simply overridden with other information.

Since I have been down that path, I am going to come back to it. Not to mention-let's not be naive, or ignorant for that matter-many of our Black brothers, and sisters are directly impacted by it. "It" being, incarceration. We can't effectively MOBilize if all of us are not a part of the MOB. As a result, let us not count out the many ex-offenders who are affected. Collateral consequences makes it difficult for several former convicts to secure the basics necessary to get back on their feet, and to properly provide for their families. They often cannot even fathom making investments in order to build something significant for the future of their lineage.

Collateral consequences are additional. They are the civil state penalties that are attached to a criminal conviction. They are separate from the direct consequences such as incarceration, fines or probation. The truth is, all these preventions often leads to desperation, and even more crime. It creates Repeat Offenders. Who needs that? These individuals directly affected don't need it, their families don't need it, and we as a people certainly don't need it! We can't be the MOB we need to be when a significant percentage of us are disfranchised.

That alone is a reason for us to ensure that we *do vote*. That alone is the reason to ensure that we MOBilize. We have to take this fight to the polls to turn things around for our incarcerated brothers and sisters. Yes, I too believe that if you do the crime, then do the time. Yet, *the time* that a great number of us are made to do is simply unjust. The rigid, "one-size-fits-all" type of sentencing laws drastically needs to come an end. This type of sentencing actually prevents judges from accurately applying the punishment to the individual, specific crime, and the circumstances surrounding it. *It has got to end. It ends with your vote!*

The Let My People Vote 2012 campaign sought to uncover some facts about how voter ID laws have specifically been used to thwart the African American vote. They shared that 25% of African Americans don't have voter IDs. Furthermore, 18% of seniors and young people were affected by voter ID laws. This campaign asserted that the law is directed to hit Democrat voters where it hurts, and like a domino effect hinders the African American vote as a result. Get this, according to the campaign the State House Majority Leader in Pennsylvania proclaimed that these voter restriction laws would allow Mitt Romney to win the state. That is huge. Despite the controversy, this organization-a MOB of sorts-dispersed this information via diverse avenues to get the word out. To wake us up.

In their view, in person voting is the last thing that can cause one party to dishonestly steal an election. This group confidently informed that the real issue are absentee ballots which can be easily stuffed. Absentee ballots are largely used by the same party who was intent on making voter ID laws a problem. Doesn't it seem like all a huge ploy? A large plan that in no way benefits us? Literacy tests, and similar nonsense roadblocks, have also been long used to hinder our vote. Why is there such a determination, such a driven force to prevent us from voting? Once again, they know our *power. The power of our vote.* Clearly it is not taken lightly. As a matter of fact, it is seen as a serious choke-hold to their agenda.

Since 2008 many states have been instituting policies in order to make it difficult for Americans to vote. These new measures have been targeted toward blacks, seniors, and the youth. They include cuts to early voting, the previously mentioned, Voter ID laws, and conducting purges of voter rolls. Purging voter rolls is the process of removing voters from voter registration lists. It is often done in secrecy, and frequently carried out erroneously. This activity is taking place around the country to SUPPRESS OUR VOTE. This is quite alarming. It's serious! On the other hand it is also quite telling that those who are establishing these regulations are aware of the power contained in our vote. They are aware of *OUR POWER*.

Voter ID laws, literacy tests, giving residents in black neighborhoods the wrong address to the polling sites, and so on is one aspect of the trouble. Though important, these tactics are only a portion of what is crippling the power of our vote. Voting has been modernized. Our vote can now be made via a computer. While this is the status of progress, it is also an opportunity for error, and for cheating to occur. I know, I know what you must be thinking. You probably want to ask me, "What the heck do you have against technology?" Well nothing really, but I do know that I can be certain that the votes can be recounted, as was the case in Florida (in the year 2000) when each Chad was recounted, if erroneous voting is suspected.

There is still one more thing. I mentioned this before, but it is worth acknowledging again. It holds a lot of weight. Many of us have jobs which stall us, even prevent us from being able to vote. That in itself is an obstacle to us exercising our power at the voting booth. Realistically, a good chunk of us cannot get to the polls on the day of the election. Those who are able to get away spend most of the time trying to get there only to stand in long lines. What has your voting experience been like? Have you been able to easily get the time to vote, and still maintain good hours at work? Okay. So the time to vote may not be an issue for you. Still, it may be a predicament for your neighbor, your cousin, your in-law. It does impact *Our Vote* significantly. We must do this thing as a MOB, remember? Our power packs a greater punch when we MOBilize. Change...Real Change begins to unfold when we show up in large numbers. With that in mind, I believe that it is critical for any election day, regardless of the level, but particularly on the national level be an official day off, across the board.

The End Result...

So with all these plans in place to keep us from casting our vote, to diminish our power, if successful we will continue to see division, breakdown and decay of our community. We will lose the ability to properly invest and build a strong future for our families. You know that American Dream that is the pride of "the man"? The American Dream that foreigners flock to the United States to achieve. The American Dream that immigrants are willing to die getting here to receive. Well, we need to take ownership of that Dream. We need to behave as though we have the very same right to the *entire* Dream, particularly since *the* Dream is possible as a result of the blood and sweat of our forefathers.

As a people it is important that we begin to fully understand, and properly use the system that our ancestors sacrificed, and fought for us to have full rights to. How long will we sit back and allow others to benefit, and to our own detriment? You may have heard it said by a senior citizen in your community, or an elderly relative, "We built this country". I agree that our sweat and blood was an ugly sacrifice which continues to leave us with the rotten end of the stick. However if we want to overcome these injustices, if we want to honor those who have gone before us, and for the sake of those who will come after us, we must begin to

54

use the system wisely. We have to be just as calculating. It is for our own good. It is for our own sake, and the sake of future African Americans.

So you have a great idea to add income to your home through your own new business. You have a burning desire to own a home. Do you know the precise laws, and requirements to start the business idea off? Do you know the exact regulations in place as it pertains to home ownership, taxes etc.? What are the laws in the neighborhood that you currently live in or in the area you would like to move to-as far as home ownership goes? Who are the leaders in your community? What are their goals, and objectives? Are you aware of potential leadership in your area who you believe can turn things around?

Being knowledgeable about all the ins and outs. Knowing the intricacies of the rules and regulations that directly affect you is of the utmost importance. I remember a time when I was not as invested. I remember when I didn't really care to understand the inner workings of the laws and how they can impact me, or my family, in one way or another. Whether jobs, investment, and even regarding the full after effects of incarceration. It is not difficult to acquire the details. There are public agencies available to us to learn the necessary information. There are programs available that we often don't take full advantage of. Something as simple as visiting the local library can make a significant difference and open us up in a new way to what we truly have access to, and the power that we are wielding in our hands.

Are you receiving a fair wage? Do you know your specific rights as it pertains the income you are due? You're not receiving your fair wage, you say? Well then, make some noise at the source. Start at the very root. Do what is available to you to change the laws. Take it to the relevant leadership. Contact your Representative, and raise the roof. I will repeat it as many times as is necessary. It has been scientifically proven that repetition leads to creating new habits. Repetition leads to mastering a new action. It is my hope that you, and I, that my people, and that we as a culture would master the action of MOBilizing to VOTE. It will make a difference to our lifestyles. It will enhance our quality of life overall. It may not occur immediately but with consistency, persistence, and tenacity, the future generations of African Americans can have another America. They can have an improved America to look forward to.

I will like to see that for my family. I will like to see that for *your family*. Hence the reason why I have personally taken the time to unearth what happens behind the scenes to affect our earning power. To discover the realities behind owning a home, and being a business owner. I have always been curious. I have always wanted to know how the "power machine" truly worked. I had an itch to raise the curtain and observe behind the scenes. I was never satisfied with what was presented on the surface. From my incarceration to today, I have used the workings of the system to catapult me to a place where I understand what the real deal is. I have worked closely with the power brokers. I have conducted my own investigations through research, and by asking all the right questions. Now I would like you to know that the "powers-that-be" will do anything to suppress, or deter your vote because that is where they can properly maintain control. That is how they will be able to maintain control of your money, maintain control of your potential investments, maintain control of your community, and neighborhood, and of our lives as a people. Our lives as an entire culture.

*Is your job satisfactory? Are you earning what you are
worth? How does this change? Vote!
You can taste ownership, but small business
regulations/red tape are standing in the way? Vote!
After laws, and taxes, does your property investment seem
more like a waste than a profit? Vote!*

The bottom-line is-and I will not be doing my job well if I
didn't repeat the simple purpose of this book-the
lawmakers, and powers that be don't think that we are
aware. They don't think that as a group, as that MOB that I
spoke about earlier, that we are knowledgeable enough to
fully understand. I mean completely grasp the POWER that
our vote holds. As a result, they seek every strategic,
justifiable, even legal loophole to keep us bound. This is
where they wield whatever power they have to NOT LET
YOU VOTE. They can do that, because they know how.
They know how to justify it. They know how to make it
sound logical, rational, and make lots of sense. Of course
they have the tools to also legitimatize any blockages. They
will put a law in place, in a heartbeat to prevent your, and
my vote.

This is where the MOB comes in. Regardless of what they
propose, or even put in to place to hinder us from voting, if
we determinably show up in large numbers. If we
relentlessly MOBilize and make our presence known to
execute our legal right despite the blockages, then there is
very little that they can do. It may seem simple, it may
seem basic but it is true, and holds serious merit. They are
threatened by our numbers, and they cannot deny us our
right to vote.

Actually, throw the problem back in to their court. Help the
powers that be, and political leaders understand that they
are creating trouble for themselves. They are inciting a

force that they may not be prepared to deal with. If you are I are continued to be disenfranchised in this way. If petty restrictions, and regulations are thrown at us to put a spoke in our wheel, there will be a bigger issue at hand, for them down the road. Naturally we will become belligerent, and refuse to comply with rules in response to their conniving actions.

Utilize your Power.
Let's utilize OUR POWER.
Local, Regional, National-whichever election,
VOTE!
Schools
Towns
Cities
States
VOTE!
Or else, gradually lose your earning Power, your investment Power, the Power to secure your families' future.

****

CHAPTER 8

MOBILIZATION

I have touched on the topic of mobilization frequently, previously. However, the subject is that much important that it does deserve its own chapter. It is necessary to highlight that once we understand why our vote does matter. Once we get how much power we possess just in the very right to vote, then we must firmly, and fully understand the need to move. We have to get there. Not just me, and not just you, *all of us*. Therefore, before I delve into the great importance, and the huge need for us to MOBilize ourselves, our families, and our communities let us take another look at the definition of MOBilize.

MOBilize:
To bring (people) ***together for action****. To come* ***together for action.***
~Merriam Webster Dictionary

Please allow me to draw your attention to the words in bold. **Together for action.** That about sums it up. We need to come together, or be brought together in order for *action* to take place. I will expound on the significance of that in a little bit. Right now, let's take a closer look at a few synonyms for the word *action*. Words that are interchangeable with that word, *action*.

<u>Action</u> =
Motion
Movement
Occupation
Power
Racket
Stir

Take a moment to carefully review the list. There's no rush, take the time to absorb each one of the synonyms.

Each of these words directly applies to what happens when we take *action* to vote *together.*

I have previously taken ample time discussing how our vote translates to Power. Action is interchangeable with Power. It is not simply my opinion, it is a fitting description detailed in the dictionary. Our English language's bible if you will. Still, I ask that we don't get caught up in the word, but in the meaning of it. Therefore, it is clear to see that our *Mobilization = Action = Power.*

Furthermore,
Mobilization = Action = Motion
Mobilization = Action = Movement
Mobilization = Action = Occupation
Mobilization = Action = Racket
Mobilization = Action = Stir

So are you ready to *Motion* toward starting a *Movement* in order to take *Occupation,* so to initiate a *Racket* and *Stir* things up? That is what is possible when we MOBilize.

According to research conducted, and included in a report published by the Washington Post, the wealthy vote more regularly, and more consistently than the young, and the poor. Unfortunately, the second half of this data adversely affects an important segment of the African American population, who are situated in that lower-income bracket. It is also quite evident that the wealthy are knowledgeable about where the power lies. They exercise their right to vote on a frequent basis. They are using the system well, and to their benefit. They know that is where the power lies, and how it is maintained. Who can blame them? They are also protecting their investments. There is no point complaining about the rich, getting richer if we are not willing to do the chief thing that can begin to loosen their firm hold on the power. It is not too late, however. That is why I am to sharing this information with you.

Still, talk is not enough. *It's time to move.* What will it take to get you out there? What will it take to get you, your family, and your neighborhood *to move*? The Washington Post also reported that individuals went out to vote in higher numbers when they received personal contact from campaigners, either person to person or via the telephone. Leading up to the 2008, and 2012 elections several volunteers reached out to people tucked away in certain African American neighborhoods that were almost forgotten. Naturally, the opposing party who felt as though this wave of outreach obstructed their agenda, used the system to thwart it. Nevertheless, personal contact with voters turned out to be very favorable for President Obama.

President Obama's second term is coming to an end. Regardless of the itty-bitty reasons why he obtained a positive outcome as a result of this type of MOBilization. Regardless of the specifics as to why he was so heavily supported by the African American community, another national-general election will be here before we know it. Are you prepared to vote, and get your family, friends, neighbors, crew etc. out to vote?

It must begin with the Primary Election. Participating in elections at every level is of the utmost importance. If you want to see changes close to home, participating in local elections is integral.
It is also important to understand every minute detail about all the candidates, and particularly the one you have got your eye on to vote for. Does their ideals match your own? What is their agenda, I mean their *real agenda*? (*Be careful not to get caught in the **Bait** and **Switch!***) What are their goals? I mentioned before that neighborhoods have lost

businesses as a result of the way residents voted. Others have depreciated, and contain dilapidated, and abandon homes, all because of a vote. I know that I keep hammering in on the same thing. However, I need to make it absolutely clear that the way one votes, or doesn't vote, can produce a detrimental outcome that maybe almost impossible to come back from.

Elections on EVERY level counts! So VOTE to avoid undesirable consequences for you, your family, and your neighborhood.

I found it very necessary to drive that point home. It is imperative that we understand that MOBilizing is not just for the big elections. The small ones also require *Motion* toward starting a *Movement* in order to take *Occupation,* so to initiate a *Racket* and *Stir* things up. These directly affect your children's schools, your homes, the aesthetics of the neighborhood, businesses in your area, and even safety. It would do us good to encourage our neighbors to vote. To help to MOBilize the neighborhood using our own personal, and direct contact. That is my objective throughout this book. I have also gone directly into communities. I take the time to talk with young men who appear to be heading down the same unfortunate path that my past did. I am hungry. I am desperate to see things turn around. I talk about our power, and the need to utilize it properly, and effectively, every chance I get. From writing this book to you, to in person interaction, to talking about this on every radio station that will have me, I need you to know that we need to *Move.* We need *Stir Things Up* with our vote.

It starts at home. Talk with every person in your household over 18 years old. Lay out the specific reasons why it is crucial that they make some noise by taking advantage of our privilege to vote at every level in this country. The privilege to decide about the School Superintendent, a mayor, a council person, a judge. These offices affect our day to day lives. Who we select can hinder or help us. Once you have spoken with your family, make use of every other platform available to you. Post one less funny video on your social media page, and get the message out about the importance of the Black vote. At the barber shop, or hair salon unashamedly let the other patrons, and workers know about the stake they have in improving the quality of life for their families, and community with their vote. Don't be afraid to take it to church, the gym, and your Greek organization, whatever it is. You are a part of this. Therefore, use whatever is available to you to MOBilize those around you.

The above strategy is useful, and will make a meaningful impact. Still, some people in our community need a slightly different approach. This is where the correct community leadership needs to come in to play. Our traditional leaders, and organizations like the NAACP, Al Sharpton and the like don't possess the influence they once did. Their message has grown weak. It has become watered down. It is as if their agenda has shifted. If we are to MOBilize every member of our community, we will need to also MOBilize those with a shady past, or even present. I am not trying to talk about my past incarceration as though it is a proud badge that I wear, but it happened. It is a reality. Another reality is that there are a host of individuals in our community who have walked that dim path, or are involved in acts that can put them there for some time. Nevertheless, the fact remains that they too have the right to vote. Drug dealers, gang members and the like, their vote counts too. Their vote added to the rest of Black community will make a noted difference. But *It has to be the right vote* though. As a result, they require the right person, the right leadership to MOBilize them. Someone who has been in their shoes. The camera ready leaders in their three piece suit wouldn't cut it for these members of our community. Oh No! New leadership is required. I will delve further into the need for new leadership later on in the book. Stay with me.

Even with my former experiences, some of the young men I have gone back into the inner city to inspire remain focused on wanting me to prove to my street credit, rather than paying attention to my message. If we are going to MOBilize every segment of the African American community, new leadership is required.

MOBilize from the inside out. Every segment of our community regardless of income, status or "past sins"-from your home to the streets-needs to come together for Action. Let's start a Movement. Let's create a Racket. Let's stir things up!

****

CHAPTER 9

Where Are the Voters Rights Organizations?

August 6th, 2015 marked fifty years since the Voting Rights Act was signed into law. It opened the door for African Americans to vote. VRA broke down legal barriers at the state and local level, providing us with an opportunity to harness our power, have a voice, or have a collective say in our future. This law did not come into being just because the government figured it was the right time. Ahead of the law being signed men, and women like you, and I took to the streets to display their displeasure with the way things were.

This cumulative show of "We're not going to take it anymore", and the tension building as a result of the consistency of black leadership reached the ears of government, and change took place 50 years ago. The infamous Bloody Sunday, the march across a bridge in Selma, Alabama, where Martin Luther King Jr., John Lewis (now Congressman, Atlanta) and other significant leaders participated, had taken place some months earlier, in March, ahead of President Lyndon B. Johnson signing the Voters Right Act of 1965. Unfortunately there are still holes in the law, and there is much work that needs to be done. There are several African Americans still disfranchised due to their criminal record. President Barack Obama and his party agrees. So does the NAACP and independent non-profit organizations who have taken up the challenge to fill those holes.

Traditional voters rights organizations like the NAACP who were once hot on the heels of the injustices against minorities, and people of color have lost their ability to penetrate our communities in a real way, in order to MOBilize our vote. Yes, their official mission remains the same in black and white (please see below) yet their reach and effectiveness has sadly diminished.

NAACP: OUR MISSION:
The mission of the National Association for the Advancement of Colored People is to ensure the political, educational, social, and economic equality of rights of all persons and to eliminate race-based discrimination.

Sounds good doesn't it? Sounds perfect actually. Still, when was the last time their mission reached your home or neighborhood, and made an impact? I had an opportunity to go in to one of the neighborhoods not too long ago. I was sharing my message and ensuring that folks were registered to vote. During my discourse I asked what they knew about the NAACP. They had no awareness of the organization, and did not feel any connectivity with them.

On the surface, to the public at large, via the media etc., they appear important. They seem integral, standing tall, and gigantic. They have come across as a force to be reckoned with when it comes to the rights of the people of color. Marches, and rallies have their merit. They draw attention. They indicate solidarity. However, this is a different time. This is the time to engage those who are directly affected by the issue. Certainly a march, and a rally can move a certain cross-section of our community, but what about really rallying *everyone*.

From talking to my neighbors, and individuals in the communities that I visit, it appears that the NAACP has been weak with getting in deep on the grass roots level. There is a new generation of voters, and a large cross section our community who will not be moved by the rhetoric from what appears to be a snobbish person in a three piece suit.

Don't get me wrong, I am not saying that an educated, well dressed and passionate civic minded person is not worthy of fighting for injustices faced by our people. No, that's not it. What I am saying however is that there is a need to get in to the trenches, and draw out all our brothers and sisters across *all* our neighborhoods regardless of background, income, criminal record etc. Some of our community want to see a face, and be able to talk to an individual who is relatable. Someone who talks their talk, and has walked their walk. This sort of person would have a better chance of making an impression, and getting results.

I shared that when I visited one of our neighborhoods, and "returned-to-the-hood" so to speak, that I was confronted by a young man who questioned me endlessly about my "street-qualifications" before he stopped to truly listen to what I was in his community to share with him. I wasn't dressed in a three piece suit, I was casually dressed but I don't look like what I have been through. If I, just a regular dude with a message, faced a challenge with penetrating this neighborhood, how much more will they be willing to listen to the lofty leadership of the NAACP?

There are other similar groups with good intentions. Let's take a look at the American Civil Liberties Union (ACLU) for example. Their mission is voting rights. According to them, they work "to protect and expand Americans' freedom to vote". As far as they are concerned, this also includes us. Yes, they've stated that "blacks voters" rights are an apart of their mission too. The ACLU is also working with a bi-partisan group in Congress to amend the Voting Rights Act to end any discriminatory changes to the voting laws. That is commendable. They are even participating in the push to end Jim Crow laws that prevent citizens with criminal records from voting. Criminal re-enfranchisement is on their "Things-To-Do" list. I applaud the ACLU for getting their hands dirty with this issue. Yet, how many of us realize that this issue minimizes the power of our people's vote. Additionally, while these laws limiting ex-convicts voting rights are on the books, we are crippled in various ways. Again, the ACLU's push is praise worthy, yet their efforts can only go so far unless there is participation on our end.

I wonder how many former criminals are aware of the work being done on their behalf to restore their right to vote. How many are able to, and even willing to lend their voice to the fight. This is where, once again, we need the right leadership to go into the deep sections of our community to draw out, educate and inspire those with a similar past, in order to MOBilize them to take up the charge, register their support and fast track the work being done at the policy level.

Have you heard of Project Vote? Established in 1994, the organization is located in Washington, DC. According to their publicly stated mission, Project Vote "works to empower, educate, and mobilize low-income, minority, and other marginalized and under-represented voters." Project Vote agrees that the black (or minority), and low-income population are somewhat strangers to the electoral process. However we are viewed as "the most vulnerable and least powerful". As a result they have taken up the fight-our fight.

I wonder. How does it feel to learn that you, your community, your people are considered vulnerable, and without power? For me, I am not comfortable with that perception. Yes, in all actually we do not overwhelming possess the same financial power of some other ethnic groups. We also do not currently have the political power we can achieve to since a sector of us are still disenfranchised, and others have not yet grasped the full measure of their vote, and therefore do not act upon it. The thing is, I believe that it all begins with our perception. How you, and I perceive ourselves as it pertains to our rights, will determine our actions. This thinking that we are weak, vulnerable, and powerless, has been thrust upon us and we have adopted it into our psyche. As a result, we walk around with the consciousness; "What's the point? My vote isn't going to make a difference anyway.", "No one cares what I think?", "One less vote wouldn't matter.", "and I'm busy. I don't have time for that." Just to name a few of our perceptions that keep a significant number of us from the polls.

Don't get me wrong, Project Vote has positioned their work well. However, my purpose is to turn our minds around. To ignite a revolution if you will. Therefore, despite what these nonprofit organizations have set out to do, we are *not* to just sit back, and watch them do the work. Let us come alongside them by keeping abreast of the issues, and lending our voices by touching base with the lawmakers in our state. Let them know that you are ready to cast your vote, and any policies standing in the way for you, or your family are unacceptable.

While organizations like the ones I have mentioned may be able to leverage their status, connections, and ability to lobby, it is integral that we come alongside them with the appropriate leadership in our communities. Leadership who can properly reach every level of our community. Leadership who speaks the language of a former felon, yet understands the needs of the homemaker. This is possible. I strongly believe that it is. But first our community must be open, and ready for it.

We *must, must, must* change how we see our own selves. We must revise how we view Voters Rights Organizations. They cannot be seen as our Savior, and we the poor, downcast, unlucky bunch. We have responsibilities. We need to open ourselves up to non-traditional, outside-the-box leadership who can truly reach our community. Do you think an Al Sharpton, or Jesse Jackson can move our core community today? I honestly do not think so. These communities will recognize any phoniness a mile away.

Let's *get hungry* about fully possessing our power, and that *power for all of us.* Government, and non-profits can only do so much but the fight isn't truly their own. *It is ours.*

Only Grassroots, 100%, "The-Real-Deal" leadership will be able to effectively motivate our neighborhoods to rally alongside the work being done by these non-profit organizations.

****

CHAPTER 10

What Happened To The Leaders Who Drove Our Voters Rights

It is clear that we do not currently have the same caliber of leaders today that we once had. Gone are the days of the Martin Luther King Jr. types. Purposeful, Driven, Single-minded, working tirelessly until the job gets done, and knowing how to properly inspire everyone around them. Even those who once made waves like Jesse Jackson, Louis Farakhan, and-pardon me as I mention him again-Al Sharpton have either grown old, given up, melted into the background, or do not still possess the same agenda, personally and publicly.

Congressman John Lewis is not as flamboyant, nor has he achieved the same type of recognition as perhaps Martin Luther Jr., Malcolm X, or even Louis Farakhan. Still he has been a consistent leader in the fight for our rights. He fought vehemently in the sixties alongside MLK. He was directly involved with voter registration. He is actually quite notable for it. As a result of his work, he was responsible for enrolling nearly four million minorities to vote. Mr. Lewis has been referred to as "the conscience of the U.S. Congress". Since he was elected to Congress in 1986, he has been a steady voice, unashamed to take a stand for what is right, and unafraid of any backlash, or even consequence. Congressman Lewis has certainly paid his dues.

During the civil rights movement, in the sixties, he endured 40 arrests, physical attacks, and several injuries. Still, undeterred, he pressed forward. John Lewis kept his eyes on the prize and accomplished what he set out to. There has been change as a result of his work. There has been progress. From then till modern day, Mr. Lewis champions the causes of our community. His approach may not be as flashy, and attract popular attention, or fame as some of our other leaders has. Today, some of our other leadership seem to be distracted by flashing television lights. It is as though they look for every excuse to jump in front of a camera. Then there are others whom have sold out their message, and activist agenda for a more comfortable existence.

There are the good guys (like the Congressman) and bad guys among our leadership. There are also those who have been labelled "bad" by our community. They have been mentally banished despite the good they have done. Do you think that Martin Luther King, Jr would have been as successful, with the Black community surrounding him as wholeheartedly, if he were leading the movement today? Do you think that with camera phones, social media apps, and 24 hour news channels that he would have been able to lead effectively despite his adulterous affairs?

I do not think so. As a people we have a tendency to view our leaders quite differently once we have learned that they have "sinned". For example Wesley Snipes was a beloved African American action figure on the big screen. He is a skillful actor, who once made the ladies swoon when he appeared on screen. However, we haven't seen him in many film roles over the last several of years. Additionally, he may have begun to loose popularity with black women as a result of his dating preferences (not dating black women), and his reasons why. Still, it was his tax evasion issues that took him over the edge. On the other hand, Robert Downey Jr. hasn't been a saint throughout his career either. Yet he rebounded wonderfully, with the overwhelming adored Iron Man character from Marvel Entertainment. Robert's past is dim in the shadows of his past while Wesley appears scared, and is not at the same level of celebrity that he once was. I'm aware that he recently turned to network television but how long has it been. How much longer was he in the celebrity "dog-house" than perhaps his white counterpart? Well, we were not generally that concerned were we?

This seems to be the pattern with African American notable figures. Regardless of whatever investment they have made, or the lives that they have been able to make an imprint upon, or change, our view of them is immediately dimmed once they have fallen in some way. The name Bill Cosby has become absolutely taboo among many African Americans today. Now, I am *not* in any way *condoning any* of the acts that he is alleged to have performed against his victims, but he has also done well in the community.

Unfortunately his "sins" now overshadow his large contributions to Historically Black Universities and

Colleges. It has been reported that he has donated more than 70 million dollars to Black Schools of Higher Education. That is a lot of money for one person, one family, to offer up for the advancement of our young people. Surely numerous lives have been impacted, even changed as a result. With so many HBCUs struggling financially, and fighting to keep their doors open, I am appreciative that Mr. Cosby had the foresight and consideration to contribute to the future of young black people. Recently, in the midst of all controversy surrounding Mr. Cosby, it has been reported that one college has distanced themselves from him as a result of the negative press surrounding Mr. Cosby, concerning alleged disgraceful attacks against women.

Again, I am not condoning any of this sort of behavior. I have a daughter, I support, and fight for the respect, and honor of all women. Still, please stay with me, I wanted to make a point about how we as Black people generally respond to the failings of our leaders which may in turn hinder their impact with the resources that they possess. Here's one other thing to consider. I have worked with billionaire Warren Buffet, and I observed that his charity giving as per his resources, do not in any way compare to Bill Cosby's.

I am writing this during the primary campaigns leading up to the 2016 Presidential Elections. Since business man Donald Trump declared his run for President he has been soaring in the polls. Despite his less than perfect character, and even faulty personal life there is a sector of this country who believe that he is saying all the right things, and has what it takes, thus far, to lead the country the way they believe it should be led. Donald Trump is now married to wife number 3, and he makes the most outrageous and politically incorrect statements. Yet the conservatives are rallying around him, and giving him the extra edge on the competition.

As far as the current Donald Trump supporters are concerned he has the ideology that can return the country to the sort of America that they believe in. A sort of America which sees the minority population as inferior, and only care to advance their own interest. They appreciate his bravado, his candor, and identify with his message. Who he is outside of that, is of little interest to them. All that matters is that he can lead them, and the country to where they want it to go. As an African American people, we are less able to compartmentalize our leaders, and separate who they are from what they can do for us. At times this can hurt what we attempt to accomplish, and even hinder progress. Back to Martin Luther King Jr. Again, think about it. If his infidelity was widely known, do you think that he would have had such faithful followers throughout the African American community? Particularly as an ordained minister. I don't think so. I hear my grandmother, and aunts cursing him out now after watching the news, and documentary pieces. The results may have been different. MLK may not have been as effective had he led us in this modern day when news breaks instantaneously.

Leaders don't need to be perfect, they need to be effective. If you're looking to someone to improve your political status, to improve your financial status, even improve your educational status, their faults should weigh so heavily into the equation that the individuals are not allowed to make an impact. It should not weigh so heavily that we invalidate, that we weaken them from being able to accomplish the job that they are perfectly suited, and ideally qualified for.

It is critical that we begin to re-think how we view leadership. Specifically as it relates to this message of harnessing our power through the right to vote. It is long overdue. I have gone on, and on about the power we possess in our vote. This power cannot be taken lightly. Whether it is a vote on your children's school board, a local, or state issue proposed on the ballot, to deciding about a state representative or the President of the United States, you have control over these decisions. You have power! In order for this power to be potent, and to have some fire behind it, *all of us must vote*. Therefore we need the right kind of leadership that can move-that can motivate all of our community, far and wide.

Al Sharpton used to be able to move a significant portion of our community. He identified with the "man-in-the-street", and spoke bravely for him. He was once a voice that the everyday black man and woman related to, and rallied around. The activist who has been referred to as a radical, and left his opposition feeling almost threatened by his delivery, has evolved into someone less effective. Of late he has reinvented himself, and become more of a savvy media figure head than a potent leader who can go into the trenches and cause change. It seems that we now have a watered version of him. Certainly the media calls upon him. Certainly they recognize him as the "voice-of-black-America". He is their sanctioned mouth piece these days. That is great for them, and even for him, but what about us? Does he truly speak for *all of us?* Okay, even if he is talking, and the words coming out of his mouth resemble our opinions. Is he the guy, the leader that we are still looking to, to make a difference where it counts for our community? Can he still reach the brother on the corner, or the cousin in lock-up? Is he really still effective?

The person who controls those with the voting power. The person who is able to mobilize the people to vote is the one who needs to lead.

I applaud the reverend for what he has accomplished, and for bringing attention to real issues that affect us. However from where I stand, himself and others who were once

"lighting stuff up" appear to have sold out. They have "sold their pass" as they say. The radical fire has burned out, and just possessing a status quo opinion appears to have taken precedent these days. Where are our leaders? What is the status of black leadership in this country? A black President does not equal black leadership. It is a great historical accomplishment, and President Barack Obama should receive honor where honor is due for his ability to run the race and win-just one term but two.

Still, once again, a black President does equal black leadership. He is the President of the United States of America. Therefore, his job is to govern the entire nation, to make plans for, and policies that affect the country as a whole. Some may argue that he has attempted to target his work toward the "little man". Wonderful! However, relying on his leadership to appropriately care for what matters to us as a people is faulty. In the words of journalist Roland

Martin, host of TV One's NewsOne Now, "The issues that matter to us, matter regardless of who is in (Presidential) office".

It is time for a new brand of black leadership. The leaders who once performed have either slowed down considerably, or lack potency. Their agenda is terribly sidetracked. They are, quite honestly, shells of their former selves. It's time for the new. New leadership. Effective leadership. Relatable leadership. When it comes to MOBilizing our people-including you and I-to recognize our power, and motivate us to *act* on it, you may be surprised to learn the sort of leadership that will be most productive. What sort of leader will move you to the polls? What sort of leader will cause you to get out and vote each time an election is called on either the local, state or national level? What sort of person can get you, and your household to take up occupation in the voting booths?

I know for me that the sort of person who can reach me, and move me, is the type of person who has been where I have been, and can talk my type of talk. Someone who can relate to me, not just because they say that they do, but they can back that up with real life experiences. I would like to remind you that a significant portion of African Americans live in inner-city neighborhoods. Close to 70 % of the black population that is. When we slice the gang membership pie, African Americans account for 35% of that populace, according to recent data from the National Gang Center. Every bit of our community needs to be properly moved if we are going to be a MOB who causes change.

This is where the correct leadership comes in. Honest leadership. Someone who tells the truth. Not someone who gives illustrious speeches which are hallow, and dull. Certainly not an individual who speaks what he or she thinks that crowd wants to hear. That only defeats the purpose of shaking us, and waking us up from the *Bait and Switch*, already being broadcast to us by politicians. A new type of leadership truly needs to rise up from among our people. An individual who has a story similar to his neighbors, but also has the crafty ability to convincingly enlighten, and stimulate the communities (or communities) to take proper possession of their rights, and privileges and embrace the power in the vote.

Sometimes cities reach out to churches to get the leadership there involved with impacting African American communities for change. Whether it be political or social change that is required, there is this thinking pattern that the Reverend or the Pastor can MOBilize the people for good, and help turn things around. While the church has been an integral part of African American history and many of its leaders have been successful with causing movement resulting in change, the intricacies of the issues that we are facing today will not be moved simply by emotional rhetoric. Church leaders do mean well, for the most part, and they sincerely want to reach back into the community using the "weaponry" that they have been trained to use for the good of the neighborhoods. Unfortunately some neighborhoods are beyond their immediate reach. Neighborhoods containing gang members, for example, will not look to a church leader to influence them about how to make their presence in the community a positive one, via their vote.

Gangs, and churches have polar opposite agendas. Furthermore, gang leaders do not carry the respect for Reverends, and Pastors that will cause them to want to accept their guidance. There is a story out of Chicago where the lawmakers offered to parole the older gang members who were in jail because the younger ones on the outside were causing havoc. It was so unbearable that the city decided to think outside-the-box in order to effect change. There is a quote that you may know. It goes something like this:

"If what you're doing isn't working, do something else."

It has been repeated so many times, and tweaked that the original author is unknown. Still you get the gist don't you?

78

I also read another one the other day that I liked very much. This author was also unknown.

"Old ways wouldn't open new doors."

That one really got me thinking. It is high time for new doors to be opened for us. I celebrate, salute, and respect what our former leaders have been able to accomplish. Our ancestors, and forefathers were soldiers marching through the fire to get to the other side for themselves, and for future generations. Now it is our time to take up the charge. Have we become too comfortable because the injustices are no longer screaming at us like segregation, and the legal inability to vote? Don't be fooled! We are not out of the woods. We've still got a long way to go. We've still got an *even better* America to fight for, for the sake of our children, grandchildren and the generations to come. Others fought so that we may have the privileges we have today. That same strength, tenacity, and ability to come together for action is already built inside of us. New leadership is required to walk us through new doors. It is time to look for leadership from new, and unlikely sources. The old is not cutting it any longer.

In Chicago, former gang leaders who have served their time, and reach back to work with current members through the anti-violence group, CeaseFire, are referred to as "Interrupters". That is an accurate description of their role, and their work. Gang members operate with a different code than the regular "John" or "Jane" in everyday life. The "Interrupters" are able to communicate in a language, or with a code that can induce the sort of action that is needed. Therefore working with these former gang leaders, or "Interrupters" can also be useful toward suitably educating this sector of our community about the power they have in the vote, instead of in the gun. It may take quite a bit of

79

work to get them to end their lifestyle as a whole, but if we can _all_-even _those of our people in gangs_-grasp this power in our vote, and MOBilize as an entire culture, well everyone else, look out!

Formal leadership dressed in a suit just will not do it right now. It is a new day. There is a need for the changing of the guards. A former gang member, or an ex-felon who has seen what they have seen, and done what they have done, but have put in the work to turn their lives around can make a very compelling leader in our urban areas, and even beyond. I have told you my story, even more than once. Since I sincerely want to get this message out, and I desperately want to impress upon our people the need to grab hold of our power by way of changing laws, and modifying policy through our vote, I have gone into our neighborhoods myself. You read the sort of welcome I received from a young man who believed that he knew more about the streets than I did. If _all of us_ are going to be sufficiently educated in order to become the sort of MOB that we frantically need to become (it is long overdue), leadership needs to be transparent, and easily recognizable.

Our traditional leaders are not what they once were, for a variety of reasons. However raising up new leadership is the key. New leadership who can look into the eye of the people, and be transparent. New leadership who understands our story, because they have lived it. The person who was a part of the problem can also be a part of the solution.

Let's look for new leadership in unexpected places. Leaders born out of the old struggle have become comfortable with their success, therefore

we need to seek leaders who are in the current struggle with us.

****

* Have you heard of an individual who has experienced this wide range of activities and is also actively involved with their community? *

CHAPTER 11

Who Is Eric Scott

In 2010 I was once told that "there are 1000 people just like me!"

The person who told me this is the Philadelphia rapper, M-Class. M-Class is not a super successful artist, but he is highly respected on the streets of Philly. When he said this to me, I was initially taken back. *A THOUSAND PEOPLE? A whole thousand? Really?* Then offense started to settle in. I began to feel insulted. This guy just basically said that I was not unique *at all*. I responded, "I know you're joking. Anyway, let me manage your music career!" His follow-up reply was, "Why?"

That conversation stuck with me until today.

In 2013 I worked on writer, Terrance Tykeem's book tour. His book dealt with the injustices that people of color continue to face in this country-the supposed "land of the free". During my time with Mr. Terrance Tykeem we visited multiple schools, churches, and radio stations. I learned quite a lot.

Terrance Tykeem and I share the same basic principles and beliefs, and we are bent on achieving some of the same goals. However, I envision a different path for accomplishing those goals. I believe that the changes we need to make to right the injustices we experience as a people of color, must come through our vote. On my last day with Terrance, just before I exited his book tour, I told him, "I am going to lead a voter registration drive."

His reply, "Why will people listen to you?" *Say What?* Again, this answer surprised me but Terrance's question in response to my question took me back to the conversation I had with M-Class, some years prior, where he told me that there were 1000 people just like me.

I have given it some thought. Some deep, long, and hard thought, and you know what? There are *not* a 1000 people just like me. Like a diamond in the dust, it is very rare to find a person who has seen the things I have, and has done the things I have done. ***Eric, right here needs more details about what you have done*** Where I have been, what I have seen, and what I have done in my entire life amounts to my capability to relate to any person in the inner city.

Here's a short list of my life experiences:
• I have been a drug dealer.
• I was once a fugitive on the run.
• I was a gang member.
• I was sentenced to prison.
• I was a hip hop artist
• I worked with many high profile music artists.
• I graduated from high school, and from college.

- I signed up, and successfully completed my US Army basic training at FT Knox, Kentucky.
- I successfully completed US Army M.O.S. training at FT Sam, Houston.
- I worked as a paralegal in the city of Philadelphia.
- I currently hold a legitimate job with a fortune 500 company.
- I have lived on the west coast.
- I live on the east coast.
- I was apart of a school tour where I informed kids about the danger of making bad decisions.

Have you heard of an individual who has experienced this wide range of activities and is also actively involved with their community? Someone who has had a dark past, risen from it, served their country, worked alongside celebrities and millionaires, and still walks through the halls of schools, and the streets of neighborhoods to pour out wisdom, knowledge, and direction about how we can possess and maintain our power as a people.

It's not arrogance. My journey tells the story itself. A story that is unfamiliar, and enables me to serve you, and our community at large to help each one realize that we are people with power. The power is in the Vote!

****

CHAPTER 12

Who We Are

According to the 2010 census, we are 37,131,771 million people strong. That accounts for 12.33% the total American population. We are the second largest minority group. Now don't let that placement phase you. The Hispanic population may out number us mathematically but they don't own the same sort of legacy that we do in this nation.

You may have heard it said that this country was built on the backs of African Americans, and that is most certainly accurate. Hence the urgency for us to utilize whatever power we have through our right to vote. Yes madam, yes sir, remember that this is your right. You inherited it! You earned it! Don't forget that as I continue to remind you, and me, just who we are. The politicians and lawmakers have been using the *Bait and Switch*, the art of *Placating*, and much *Trickology*-among other things-to keep us psychologically bound us for years. Still, even they know the reality; that they have profited off of our sweat, and blood. Back in 2012, Filmmaker Michael Moore was quoted saying, "This is a nation founded on genocide, and built on the backs of slaves." It was recorded on CSPAN at the time. Naturally his white counterparts dismissed it as Moore being controversial, liberal, far left etc.

Musician Bob Dylan has also claimed that America will never be able to rid themselves of the shame of "being founded on the black of slaves." It doesn't appear that the lawmakers are feeling any shame regarding this truth. If they did they wouldn't be feverishly working to suppress our vote. State after state, action has been taken to disable us from being able to walk in the fullness of our rights, and-what they absolute don't want us to realize-the fullness of our power. We can't afford to let them do this anymore.

For years they infiltrated our neighborhoods with cocaine and guns, determined to keep us oppressed. I fell victim to this strategic ploy. It was a form of control. We could be just as successful, just as healthy, just as free as they would allow us, and no more. Hence the large number of African Americans incarcerated. Again, this type of abuse. Yes I said it; *abuse*. This type of abuse would not be warranted if government felt secure, or the country was not still steep in racism. This is an unfortunate fact that we have to face.

I listened to a news radio program the other day and I was reminded that following the desegregation of schools in the sixties, neighborhoods began to blend. However, segregation returned in the eighties and nineties when each racial group began to find their respective corners again. It was as though once the neighborhoods became too populated with African Americans, others retreated. Additionally, the current state of gentrification in New York, Washington D.C., Philadelphia and other urban cities is very telling of how our homes, and our existence is of minimal concern. Although some cities tried to work with the present Black population to transition the areas, unless you are a home owner you could be gradually squeezed out.

On this same radio news program, the host interviewed the leader of Singapore. He asked him what he thought was Singapore's greatest accomplishment. This President responded that their social relationships was their proudest accomplishment. He declared that the country developed knowing that it inhabited a mixture of cultures, and devised the education system, and housing to encourage cultural mixing, understanding, and toleration.

I am not proposing that we hop, jump and adopt this format. However, I do believe that we-as a country as a whole-can stand to humble ourselves and pause to realize that if we want race relations to work, that with the due diligence of everyone, it is possible. I am a huge proponent of learning from others. As a matter of fact, the desire to know how the true American "system" worked and how the other side was benefiting from it is what led me to position myself alongside key individuals, make the right connections, then circle back to bring it to our homes, and our lives. Still, this sort of change-equivalent to what Singapore's experiencing-can only be possible when minds are changed. When thought patterns, and beliefs make a 180 degree transition. I do find that hard to come by, not from us, but from those who are bent on rendering us powerless.

The recent, and frequent police brutality incidents are an indication that old mindsets are rooted deep, and are difficult to break. Not to mention the variety of ugly racial comments that have been spouted about the President since Barack Obama took office. The number of messages, and social media posts were so terrible, particularly after the 2012 election, that the media gathered them and broadcasted them via both the television and print broadcast news. I mean, I didn't expect the entire nation to be on board with his victory. Of course not. Many people voted for the other guy. Still, I didn't expect the comments to be so downright foul in the 21st century. These opinions reflected mindsets so archaic, it reminded me of the ideology of the slave owners.

There are those who are determined to continue to thrust the idea upon us, that we are inferior to them. Regardless of how far we have come, they want us to remain politically, financially, and socially crippled. In spite of this, in the words of the deceased Maya Angelou (May she rest in peace) "Still I Rise"---"Still We Rise"! Regardless of what we have been subjected to, we continue to rise. Slavery, Jim Crow, Civil Rights, the Government's plot to weaken us via planting drugs in our neighborhoods, suppressing our vote...through it all, *We Continue to Rise.*

Among all the other minority groups, we are the first to have a black president at the helm. Although that maybe the most glaring achievement these days, we have acquired several others throughout the centuries. I would like to take this time to go down memory lane. To remember some soldiers who didn't allow their current circumstances to dictate what they would attain to, and deter them from establishing a legacy for the generations to follow. If you think that we have it hard now, and are experiencing injustices against us-and yes, we are-they still cannot compare to the hardships faced by these brave trail blazers:

- 1821 - First African American to hold a patent: *Thomas L. Jennings*, for a dry-cleaning process.
- 1836 - First African American elected to public office and to serve in a state legislature: *Alexander Twilight*, Vermont.
- 1865 - First African-American attorney admitted to the bar of the U.S. Supreme Court: *John Stewart Rock.*
- 1870 - First African American to vote in an election under the 15th Amendment to the United States Constitution, granting voting rights regardless of race: *Thomas Mundy Peterson.*
- 1919 - First African-American special agent for the FBI: *James Wormley Jones.*
- 1921 - First African-American woman to become an aviation pilot, first American to hold an international pilot license: *Bessie Coleman.*
- 1938 - First African-American female federal agency head: *Mary McLeod Bethune* (National Youth Administration).
- 1950 - First African American to receive a "lifetime" (officially "during good behavior") appointment as

federal judge: *William H. Hastie*, U.S. Court of Appeals for the Third Circuit.

- 1950 - First African-American woman to compete on the world tennis tour: *Althea Gibson.*.
- 1964 - First African-American pilot for a major commercial airline: *David Harris*, American Airlines.
- 1965 - First African-American U.S. Air Force *General: Benjamin Oliver Davis, Jr.* (Three-star General).
- 1966 - First African-American coach in the National Basketball Association: Bill Russell (Boston Celtics).
- These are the highlights. This list can go on for pages.

Did you enjoy that? I hope that you at least appreciated it. This list wasn't meant to bore you but outside of the well-known, and much talked heroes such as Fredrick Douglas, Jackie Robinson, Marian Anderson, Thurgood Marshall, Martin Luther King, and so on. I thought it necessary to point out everyday heroes who carved their own path in the face blatant racism and legal injustices, and disgustingly unfair treatment. The circumstances surrounding their lives were not comparable to our lives today. Yes, many of us endure valid, and significant struggles these days. I also agree that blatant injustices are still occurring in 2015. Yet the conditions under which we are experiencing our travails do not compare to the conditions that existed for individuals in history. They did not possess any of the rights, and privileges we have today. They lacked protection in the form of laws, and would be arrested or harmed for entering food establishments, entertainment halls, or movie theaters. Their lives were limited in so many ways. They press forward, and pressed on nevertheless.

As we look back at the past, it is also very important to look ahead to our future. A very big part of our future are our children, and grandchildren. It is crucial that we understand the immediate necessity to strip away at the laws, and policies that will affect them negatively. That will negatively affect our people's future. Let's continue to rise like Maya Angelou. Let's rise, not just for ourselves, but also for our children. My children certainly give me the motivation to press this message forward. It is also *all our children* who drives me to speak at schools. As I work to paint a realistic picture for them about the true nature of progress, and overcoming obstacles that will try very hard to work against them, you, and your neighborhoods can become more in tuned with "the system", how it truly works. Use it to your advantage and act to turn things around, one vote at a time.

Take a look at what is happening to our children around the country now. Young men are being treated brutality by police officers. Our young men and women are judged, and sentenced harshly for petty crimes. Time after time I have listened to parents who are anxious about the safety of their sons, not because they are involved in illicit activity but because of the apparent attitudes toward young black men by law enforcement. Even women are in jeopardy of this sort of unfair treatment.

As a result, African-American parents are growing more and more anxious about the safety of all their children in this country in which everyone is supposedly equal. I know you are frustrated, even angry about the status of this issue. I am as well. You know I have had my own run-ins with law enforcement. I know the full measure of what they are capable of. Nevertheless, if you want to get them where it hurts. If you want the police to stand up, and take notice as well as tie their hands firmly, take the necessary steps to change the laws by voting.

Do you know that President Obama declared that if a police officer is fired as a result of excessive force or misconduct, the police department is also within their right to decertify the officer? This disables them from being able to get another job in that profession. However, not every state has made this act mandatory, and reckless cops are allowed to get jobs elsewhere, at another precinct, town, state etc. For the sake of your children, let's *be proactive, not reactive.* Demand that this become law, and be mandatory across the country. For the sake of your children, do the due diligence.

Remember my talking about our white brothers, and sisters and how they spring into action immediately in order to change anything they don't like? We often size them up from a distance. We outwardly criticize their characteristics, yet inwardly desire a fuller life similar to their own. They fully understand their rights, and the power they wield as citizens of this democracy. Their forefathers established the formula, and their parents educate them at home, teaching them to take complete ownership of it.

We too need to take complete ownership of our rights. Our own forefathers literally worked themselves to the bone for us to take ownership of our rights. What would you have done if you were in their shoes? In the 40s, 50s, 60s, you would have taken on the attitude too, "oh, hell no, we're not going to take this anymore." However today, the fight doesn't simply work by taking it to the streets with a large march or rally. We win this round of the fight by demanding changes to laws. Again I repeat strategically. Repetition is a tool toward mastering whatever we are re-training our minds to do. Therefore once more, *demanding changes to the laws is where the real power lies.* We achieve that by *all* of us *coming together* for *action.* By MOBilizing, becoming a MOB. Infiltrate your state representative's space. State after state, after state, let them know we mean business.

What is happening in the schools? Is the quality of education minimized due to lack of funds which are being filtered elsewhere, and wasted? There is deliberate strategy where Prices on items are marked up, and taxes are attached to anything possible with the claim that it is going to be applied to the schools. What really happens is that we don't pay close attention to where the funds truly go, and in the end the schools don't see a single bit of it. As a result, the money is squandered. Be conscientious. Begin now. Don't allow the **Bait** and **Switch** to continue to control us. To control our children's future. Instead take the control back.

Begin to be particularly aware of how funding is being allocated. This impacts your personal finances, ability to properly save and your children's future. Start today! Learn the specific office in your city, or state, which has the answers you need. Get your questions ready, and take the control back. Refuse to be **Placated**, and demand that **Trickology** keeps its distance. Don't just accept what you've been told. You're in charge of your children's future.
It is also critical that you educate your children like it were yesterday. Begin to explain to them that although injustices do exist for them as African-Americans, in this democratic nation of the United States of America, their responsibility is to know their rights and embrace their privilege to demand changes to laws, with their vote. If they are to overcome obstacles, unfair treatment, and the like they must become knowledgeable about all their rights in every circumstance. Explain that the powers that be sit in their lofty offices expecting us to be dumb, deaf, and stupid, and not aware of the policies, regulations, laws, and taxes that adversely affect us. They also wait for us to react to every

91

unfair situation with violence so their law enforcers can slap handcuffs on us, and throw us in jail for unjust lengths of time. Instead, because we've enlightened them, they will discover a smarter, more informed, and sharp generation. What a different African American community we will be, if the next generation fully embraced this right. Like a fresh breeze, it can turn us around. It can turn things around.

What about our neighborhoods? Have you truly considered how your voting decisions have affected the development or the decline of your neighborhood? Sometimes we don't really know what we are voting for when we read a particular issue listed on the ballot. Hence the importance to look behind the title of the issue, and learn the exact ramifications.

If local government is proposing a new, fancy, and cushy recreational facility, don't get so hung up on the new "shiny" item that you have not investigated where the money is specifically coming from to pay for the swanky facility. Do you make decisions about other areas of your life without first knowing about the issue from all sides? How is that working for you? One New Jersey community did something similar to the example mentioned above. They acquired a new skating rink, which they overwhelmingly voted for, but loss so much more in critical services for the neighborhood, and for their families.

As far as neighborhoods go, it is time to view them collectively. As we look ahead toward creating a better future for our children remember that we must *come together for action*. We must MOBilize. Therefore, it is difficult to do so if we continue to maintain our tribalism mentality. Being concerned with "my hood", and "my hood" only is a threat to the impact of OUR VOTE. It is a threat to our effectiveness, and to our success. I recall the

2008 election. Volunteers came out of the wood works to register voters, and voters showed up in droves, from every area, with one goal in mind. This is the sort of energy that is needed for each election, at *every level*, and beyond a qualified black candidate being on the ticket.

Please be reminded of the earlier quote from journalist Roland Martin. Our issues matter regardless of who is the Presidential Candidate. I will extend that to our issues matter regardless of who is running for mayor, regardless of who is vying to be on the city council, regardless of who is campaigning to be elected Governor, Senator etc. Our Issues ALWAYS Matter, and therefore **OUR VOTE** *ALWAYS* **MATTERS!**

****

www.ingramcontent.com/pod-product-compliance
Lightning Source LLC
Chambersburg PA
CBHW060436290526
45791CB00002B/957